GENERALS FOR PEACE
AND DISARMAMENT

D1195019

The USSR in its global setting

GENERALS FOR PEACE
AND
DISARMAMENT

A Challenge to US/NATO Strategy

Introduction by Brigadier Michael N. Harbottle
Foreword by Admiral Gene R. La Rocque, USN (Retd.)

UNIVERSE BOOKS

NEW YORK

Published in the United States of America in 1984
by Universe Books
381 Park Avenue South, New York, N.Y. 10016

© English edition Berg Publishers Ltd 1984
Copyright © 1983 by Hoffmann und Campe Verlag, Hamburg

All rights reserved. No part of this publication
may be reproduced, stored in a retrieval system, or
transmitted, in any form or by any means, electronic,
mechanical, photocopying, recording, or otherwise,
without prior permission of the publishers.

84 85 86 87 88/10 9 8 7 6 5 4 3 2 1

Printed in Great Britain

Library of Congress Cataloging in Publication Data
Main entry under title:

Generals for peace and disarmament.

Authors: Gert Bastian, and others.
1. North Atlantic Treaty Organization—Military policy
—Addresses, essays, lectures. 2. Atomic weapons—Addresses,
essays, lectures. 3. Peace—Addresses, essays,
lectures. 4. Disarmament—Addresses, essays, lectures.
I. Bastian, Gert. II. Harbottle, Michael.
UA646.3.G344   1984   355'.03304   84-40351
ISBN 0-87663-447-1
ISBN 0-87663-862-0 (pbk.)

Contents

Editorial Note

'Generals for Peace and Disarmament' is a group of former NATO generals and admirals who first came together in 1981. They are united by the similarity of their views on the dangers inherent in the nuclear arms race, the absolute necessity of arms limitation in addition to disarmament, and on questions of European security.

Over the past few years the group has made repeated statements on the problems of security, in, for example:

— a memorandum addressed to the 1981 Madrid Conference on European Security and Co-operation;

— a memorandum to the Foreign and Defence Ministers and senior officers of the NATO countries, in November 1981;

— a memorandum to the delegations attending the Second UN Special Session on Disarmament, in June 1982.

The group consists of the following: General G. Bastian (FRG); General J. Christie (Norway); Marshal F. da Costa Gomes (Portugal); Brigadier M.N. Harbottle (Great Britain); General G. Koumanakos (Greece); General Joao Lima (Portugal); General M. Herman von Meyenfeldt (Netherlands); General A. Papaspyrou (Greece); Admiral M. Papathanassiou (Greece); General N. Pasti (Italy); Admiral A. Sanguinetti (France); General M. Tombopoulos (Greece) and General G. Vollmer (FRG).

During their second meeting, which took place in Vienna at the end of 1982, the group discussed the present book (which was first published in Germany in 1983), in which they give their views on some of the most fundamental questions of war and peace in our time.

Editorial responsibility for this present edition lies with General Bastian, Marshal da Costa Gomes, Brigadier Harbottle, General von Meyenfeldt and General Tombopoulos.

Foreword

Many military men on both sides of the Atlantic have long realized that the use of the nuclear weapons entrusted to their care would destroy the world. Now in its first English-language edition, this book by the group known as Generals for Peace and Disarmament traces the thoughts of several NATO flag officers as they join to oppose the introduction of more nuclear weapons in Europe. This is an important statement by men who have been responsible for the defence of their countries. In their long and varied careers, they have all reached an inescapable conclusion: There is clearly no military use for weapons that will inevitably destroy all that is worth defending.

Many of us began our careers before the invention of the atomic bomb. In those days, rational men could still contemplate war as the last resort in the defence of one's country. As military men, we felt it was our duty to fight and win those wars.

But winning a nuclear war is not possible. Contrary to the claims of President Reagan and the 'Star Wars' advocates, there is no defence against these weapons. No matter how nearly perfect a defence might be, its penetration by just a small fraction of the 20,000 strategic warheads already available would kill millions of people.

Over the last thirty-five years, the destructive potential, complexity, and number of these weapons has grown astronomically. Both civilian and military analysts have spawned a whole new language surrounding the discussion of these weapons. Acronyms like MIRV or MAD and catch phrases like 'counter-force' and 'flexible response' hide the terrible realities of these weapons. As military men who have spent our lives working with these weapons, we have a duty to translate this jargon into language that everyone can understand. Generals for Peace and Disarmament has taken a step in this direction. It is clear that no matter how many acronyms or catch phrases are used, planning for nuclear war is preparing for the death of hundreds of millions of people and our civilization.

Today, generals and admirals in the United States, United Kingdom, France, China, and the Soviet Union are actually planning, training, arming, and practising for nuclear war — a war no one wants; a war we cannot win; a war we probably cannot survive.

The statements of the Generals for Peace and Disarmament have their roots in the cold logic of the military professional as did General Eisenhower's comments of twenty years ago: 'All war is vulgar and ugly. Nuclear war is insane'. General Sherman spoke for many of us who have seen the face of battle when he said: 'War is hell'.

Gene R. La Rocque
Rear Admiral, USN (retd.)

Introduction

This book reflects the broad consensus of views of a group of retired generals and admirals from various NATO countries — a group drawn together by their deep concern at what they perceive to be a misplaced and dangerous strategy pursued by their respective governments within the NATO alliance.

It is not usual for military men, brought up in the ingrained traditions of loyalty, to challenge government policy so publicly. Some members of the group have come to their critical attitude since their retirement. Others have had the courage to retire on a matter of principle, so vigorously do they consider present NATO policies to be fundamentally wrong, dangerous and often based on deception.

The book may appear to some conservatively minded readers as an apologia for the USSR and its allies, and gratuitously anti-American. But that is not what is in our minds. We are simply expressing opinions which are held equally strongly by many in the USA itself, and increasingly by individuals formerly in the highest echelons of government, who are also voicing their concern and revulsion for policies they perceive to be dangerous and wrong.

In writing this book, members of the Generals for Peace and Disarmament group have attempted to present motives and reactions, cause and effect; not to denigrate in a negative frame of mind. Besides analysing the present dangerous situation that exists between the two main alliances in Europe, we have also tried to paint a hopeful picture, tracing the painfully slow progress in creating an international code of behaviour and a blueprint for international security in one treaty after another. Presenting them as we have, we invite the reader to view them as we do — as construction blocks in the edifice of 'confidence building', which has been the declared intent of member States of the United Nations but which governments, particularly those of the West, so capriciously have ignored.

As our analysis develops, we have been forced to question motives, so contrary does the behaviour of the Western side appear. Why should Cruise and Pershing II missiles have been deployed in Western Europe when both weapons continue to be notoriously unreliable in their tests (26 per cent and 30 per cent failure rate respectively)? Why should the public have been fed with deliberate falsification of the reason for their deployment — to counter the USSR SS-20s — when General Bernard W. Rogers, Supreme Allied Commander Europe, has himself declared in evidence to the US Senate's Armed Services Committee (13 March 1983) that 'most people believe it was because of the SS-20 that we modernized. We would have modernized irrespective of the SS-20 because we had this gap in our spectrum of defense developing and we needed to close the gap'. Why deliberately deploy these weapons when the threatened consequence of doing so would mean a Russian walk-out from the Geneva INF negotiations linked with a retaliatory deployment response, and then express surprise and hurt feelings when it happens? Such a deliberate choice of cause-and-effect only exacerbates the already strained relations between the two super-powers; strained because of the rising fear and distrust and a complete absence of intent to listen when either side makes any constructive suggestion.

The frontispiece to the book is a map of the world as viewed from the North Pole. This is the map you find most commonly in Russia and it illustrates only too clearly the geo-political perspective that Russia has of its strategic and security position in the world. It is not difficult to appreciate from this perspective how completely encircled and targetted the Russians feel and how this preys on their sense of fear and distrust of the Western nations' intentions against them. Is it to be wondered at that the Soviet Union sees the arms race and nuclear deterrence in a far starker light than we do in the West? The perspective of the world as viewed by the West is quite different. Shown as a flat montage in our atlases, it displays no geo-political dimension, except to show Russia as a dominating land mass towering over the whole of Asia and most of Europe. It is important to interpret these respective perspectives properly for they influence the perceptions which we have of the 'enemy'. It is time that we stood in each other's shoes and took a long, hard look at how the one sees the other. In this critical analysis of the policies and strategies of NATO, the book focuses on the way in which hardline and mistaken

[4]

perceptions have influenced the decisions which have led us to the dangerous confrontation which threatens us now. It is time that we all, on both sides of the ideological divide, reassessed those perceptions and studied more carefully the basis for our respective fears and the validity of the perceived threat.

The book makes the point that too much policy domination by the United States has emasculated the control that its Western European allies have over their individual as well as their collective security. European unity in the NATO context is still a goal. While it remains unrealized, the role of the United States in European affairs will continue to be overriding. Yet the heritage and destiny of Europe belongs to all Europeans, east and west. It is a responsibility to be shared and a determining factor in whether Europe will become a continent of peace or remain a potential battleground.

We in the Generals' Group for Peace and Disarmament came together as a working group in 1981, after the publication of the book *Generale für den Frieden,* an anthology of our recorded views on European security. The group meets regularly and its members have individually or collectively taken part in a series of programmes and activities in all parts of the world in support of the international peace movement. In 1982, it was decided that we should attempt to arrange a meeting between ourselves and a comparable group of senior military officers from the Warsaw Pact countries. In May 1984, that meeting took place in Vienna at which there was a representative from all seven of the East European countries and from six of the West. The meeting of generals was unprecedented. Its purpose was not only to initiate a dialogue between military men which would allow experienced soldiers to consider the serious issues threatening world peace and how these might be resolved, but also as a confidence building initiative. The concluding Statement, agreed by all present, can be found as Appendix 1 at the end of this book. The importance of such meetings should not be ignored for they are relevant to what this book has to say; that only through a total willingness by all concerned to end the arms race and to work purposefully for a mutual and progressive disarmament programme can we hope to remove the threat of nuclear annihilation. But fundamental to the whole process must be the willingness to communicate; for only through communication can confidence be built and distrust removed. The initiative of the Generals in Vienna in May 1984 was a contribution to that communication-confidence building process.

[5]

The Final Document of the First UN Special Session on Disarmament in 1978 (later to be endorsed at the Second Special Session of 1982) stressed that 'the decisive factor for achieving real measures of disarmament is the political will of States'. What this book argues is that the necessary 'political will' is lacking in today's strategy and purpose and is missing from the disarmament talks; and that it is NATO which has failed most in this respect.

We will no doubt be accused of taking a one-sided position and of ignoring the culpability of the Soviet Union. There are always two sides to any dispute and the Soviet Union bears its share of responsibility for the situation in which this world finds itself. But this book, which is the first of two (the second is to be published in 1985), is concerned with the NATO side of the problem and what we see as being a dangerous and disruptive policy on the part of the United States in particular, and of NATO in general; for it disregards the urgent need for positive and genuine arms negotiation initiatives as a means of structuring an acceptable degree of security for all without the constant threat of nuclear war.

This book is an exposé of the self-deception of US/NATO strategy. It underscores the motives which have dominated US political thinking in the four years of the Reagan Administration and throws into sharp focus the tug of war between US political policy and NATO's military strategy. But above all, the book demonstrates the world of nuclear fantasy in which the United States and possibly to a lesser extent her NATO partners exist. Perhaps we should have entitled this book *Allies in Wonderland*.

Michael Harbottle

[6]

Generals for Peace
and Disarmament: a Survey

> I believe that the growing strength of the movement
> against nuclear war will be the most impressive
> phenomenon of the 1980s.
>
> *George F. Kennan*
> Former US Ambassador to USSR 1952-3

New and better ways

It created some surprise and speculation when in 1981 a book entitled
Generals for Peace was published, in which we, former generals and
admirals of NATO countries, outlined our views on the East–West
confrontation and the threat that nuclear weapons and the nuclear
deterrent strategy posed to East–West security, thus aligning ourselves
with the growing world-wide movement for disarmament. Not
surprisingly, it gave rise to questions about our sympathies and motives
but the answer is very simple — we are concerned, like many millions
around the world, about the chances of survival of our civilization and
the fate of our people. Our military experience and knowledge of war
has led us to the conviction that the nuclear arms race is a hazard to the
survival of mankind.

The arms race has been with us for over a generation and has
reached frightening dimensions. It has created much prejudice. It has
given birth to a continuous debate as to the conceptual validity and
professional ethics of nuclear arms, not only among the military but
also among government representatives, politicians, scientists,
armament manufacturers, strategists, writers, journalists and, not
least, the general public but, despite this, military and political

[7]

strategies have continued to be based predominantly on nuclear weapons. More and more scientific, technological, political and financial resources have been, and still are being, provided to fuel the nuclear arms race instead of controlling it. It is our resolve to work to halt this dangerous process, striving first to reduce and finally to eliminate the threat of a nuclear holocaust. There is no doubt that it represents the most crucial problem facing the world today. It is a problem requiring commitment and inspiration. Faced with this genuine concern, the insinuations that the opponents of the nuclear arms race are the victims of Soviet propaganda or, worse, are the 'stooges' of the Soviet Union, are narrow-minded and malicious. It is not a case of either the American or the Soviet way of life, only a choice between life and death.

It is inconceivable and somehow inexcusable to some that military officers should oppose the arms race and attack the military barriers it creates in international relations. The fact that we base what we believe on our appreciation of current political developments, and the increasing potential for military conflict, does not excuse us in their eyes. Our critics call into question our credibility and would, no doubt, wish to denigrate what we express in this book. However, politically objective and unbiased reviewers of this book, who have made a serious evaluation of its contents, have commented favourably on our resolve to 'stand up to be counted' and on our military competence to publish our views. The book has been described as an 'initiative from an unexpected quarter and an encouragement to those living under the threat of nuclear war'.[1]

We and other soldiers who have reached the same or similar conclusions are often asked, in a somewhat reproachful way, why senior military experts start considering military plans and developments in a more critical light only after their retirement. Indeed, when the 'father of the US nuclear submarine fleet', Admiral Hyman G. Rickover, announced: 'I am not proud of the role I played. I would rather send all nuclear ships to the bottom of the sea',[2] he shocked many people. In the past it was quite common for retired military commanders to find the time and leisure, as well as the personal impartiality necessary, to look back over their lives and to publish memoirs. Today, however, the pace and outcome of developments in military technology are increasing the dangers of the arms race and mean that the military commander has a greater responsibility towards society. The possibility of actually having to use armed

[8]

forces in war compels him to consider the nuclear option while he is still in active service. He has to make a decision for or against the nuclear arms race. General Bastian provides an example of this kind of decision — in his capacity as a divisional commander of the German Bundeswehr, he voiced his reservations about NATO's decision to deploy American medium-range missiles in Central Europe in a letter to the then West German Minister of Defence, Hans Apel. Another example is General Herman M. von Meyenfeldt who, in 1971, ten years before his retirement, tried to have a proposal on the non-first use of nuclear weapons incorporated into the programme of the political party in Holland to which he belongs. General Nino Pasti (Italy) said of himself:

> I am perhaps a somewhat untypical general. Even during my active service in the Italian Army and with NATO, I was always advocating that East and West should get to know each other better. While working for NATO, I came to the conclusion that there are too many nuclear weapons stationed in Europe and I drew up reports in which I outlined my views. I may not have been able to achieve my goal, that is, to reduce the number of nuclear bombs in Europe, but at least I have prevented other military men from doubling them.[3]

Nino Pasti pointed out that a critical attitude towards nuclear armament, as well as a call for the reduction of nuclear capabilities, are not advocacies for rendering NATO countries defenceless.

Georg Paul Hefty, writing in the *Frankfurter Allgemeine Zeitung*, said: 'What the retired generals and admirals have to say about the defence of peace in Europe is dominated more by their personal commitment than by their grasp of security policy issues'.[4] We do not question Herr Hefty's capacity for judging the ins and outs of security policy but, so far as the group of generals is concerned, their competence to understand the situation is well founded — unless of course people wish to suggest that the governments of several NATO countries were ill-advised in appointing them to their NATO posts. All of us have studied and experienced both the theoretical and the practical aspects of warfare over decades in senior military positions. We have served our countries as officers in various capacities and we have performed a variety of senior staff appointments. Among our ranks there are generals and admirals who have served at HQ, as directors of military training, as military policy advisers to ministers, one has been deputy

[9]

to the NATO Supreme Commander for Europe responsible for nuclear planning and last, but certainly not least, as a Head of State (Portugal's Marshal da Costa Gomes). Thus we have held posts which have allowed us to gain the political experience necessary to evaluate the crucial issues of our time regarding war and peace and to suggest possible solutions. The difference between us and our former colleagues, who do not share our convictions, is that we have drawn political conclusions from our experiences, rejected the whole concept of nuclear weapons and aligned ourselves to the peace movement.

After the publication of *Generale für den Frieden* in 1981, we came together as a working group and since then have prepared and submitted a number of memoranda in which we have presented our case for a change in current armament policies and made proposals for the maintenance of peace through a programme of disarmament. In this repect, under the collective title of 'Generals for Peace and Disarmament', we have undertaken both together and individually initiatives to further our efforts in support of peaceful relations between nations. Among those to whom we have addressed our views are those international committees which we thought particularly suited and competent to serve this end. In 1981, we sent memoranda to the Madrid meeting of the Conference for Security and Cooperation in Europe and, in the same year, to the Conference of NATO's Foreign and Defence Ministers at The Hague. In 1982, we delivered a memorandum to the United Nations' Second Special Session on Disarmament. We believe that by doing this we have been able to support the development of the peace movement whose influence, cultural and religious, is and must continue to be of major importance in persuading governments from taking and implementing decisions which would lead to further escalations of the arms race and in ensuring that our world is made free from the threat of war.

War philosophies for the dustbin of history

Today, people are dominated more by their anxiety about the prospect of a nuclear war than by the fact that it can be avoided. Even military experts and security policy makers find it difficult to see a way of breaking out of the vicious circle of peace–war–peace–war which has characterised history since the beginning of time. Our generation joined the armed forces, either just before or during the Second World

War. The basic military principle of that time was that it was every government's duty to use military force to safeguard national interests (which did not mean only defending a country against a threatened invasion of its territory). It was the task of the leadership, and particularly of the generals, to keep themselves and their armies in a state of readiness in case of war.

Regardless of where the members of the group Generals for Peace began their military careers, their views were formed by the same models of the origin and nature of war. It is not the intention of the Generals to analyse the degree to which various war philosophies influenced the different countries but their views at that time were influenced by the philosophical but stereotyped concepts which permeated military thinking in different countries. Among these were that:

(i) war was a natural state and an immutable law in the history of mankind, something decreed by fate or, as the English military historian, J.G. Fuller, put it, a 'dominant factor' in history;

(ii) war was the result of man's 'instinctive' aggressiveness originating in 'the depths of the human soul';

(iii) natural philosophies claimed that war was a product and a regulator of the 'over-population' of the earth. In 1945, the American Hessler described the atom bomb as 'a potential technological means of regulating the population';[5]

(iv) war was justified as a means of wiping out those states or political organisations which were deemed 'inferior' by race, creed or colour;

(v) the causes and objectives of war explained in geo-political terms. Annexation and colonial conquests were prepared for by the claim that 'new *Lebensraum*' was needed;

(vi) war was quite simply a part of 'God's world order'.

War was thus presented as something natural, to be taken for granted and which needed to be prepared for both conceptually and militarily, as it was in Germany and Italy before 1939. But even more than the philosophy of war, the political doctrines and the prevailing strategic theories of the prewar period influenced warfare and, consequently, our own experience of war. Included among these doctrinal theories were:

— the Italian General Giulio Douhet's theory of air warfare. Over-estimating the capabilities of the recently created air forces, he put forward the view that, in establishing air superiority over the

[11]

enemy, the bombing of towns and industrial centres in the enemy's hinterland would be the decisive factor in influencing the outcome of a war. These ideas had a significant influence on strategic thinking in Germany, Great Britain and the United States, finally leading to the strategy of terror bombing in the Second World War;

— the concept of total war. The First World War German General, Erich Ludendorff, was the most prominent representative of this line of thought. He advocated a concept of extreme destruction which called for warfare not only against the armed forces of the enemy but also against the whole of enemy society. The population was not to be spared — parts of it might be totally wiped out. The leadership of the German *Wehrmacht* applied these principles in a most barbarous fashion by issuing the 'Under-cover-of-night Decree' and the 'Commissar Order' which led to the murder of defenceless prisoners of war;

— the colonial wars, fought by Britain and France in the eighteenth and nineteenth centuries and, at a slightly later date, by Italy, were often brutal and savage, against poorly-armed 'rebel' forces. These wars led the European nations to a conceptual approach to colonial law-and-order operations in the twentieth century which relied upon enforcement action as the means for putting down those who, by seeking self-determination and independence, were adjudged a threat to the security of the colonial system.

If one also takes into account the facts that war was glorified as 'the most important stimulus for human progress'[6] and that nationalist hero worship was encouraged, it is not difficult to see how patriotic and eager young officers could be motivated to devote all their energies to wars that served neither to defend their countries nor protect the life and property of their own people.

We were active participants in the Second World War. Some of us fought in the vast territories of the Soviet Union and in the deserts of North Africa; some participated in naval battles in the Atlantic and Pacific Oceans; some belonged to patriotic underground forces in Western Europe and fought for the freedom of the European peoples from Nazi oppression; some also served in the last colonial actions of this century, in Algeria, Angola, Cyprus and Mozambique. Last, but not least, some participated in the UN peacekeeping operations designed to pacify without force of arms dangerous conflict situations.

As members of that generation, we have been deeply influenced by

[12]

our own personal experiences of war and its effects upon us. They have caused some of us to start thinking about the real causes of war and about the prospects of avoiding fresh military conflicts in the future. The fundamental dictum that war is 'the continuation of politics by other means' was not generally appreciated by the military, although the Prussian military theoretician, General Karl von Clausewitz, came to that conclusion 150 years ago. This lack of historical knowledge has in part been corrected by the political character of the Second World War and the course of international politics since.

During the Second World War, the soldiers and officers in the armies allied against Hitler had the satisfaction of knowing that they were fighting for the noble cause of freedom from oppression. Members of the Fascist *Wehrmacht*, on the other hand, had to bear the moral stigma of having participated in a war aimed at enslaving all the peoples of Europe. If they were not directly guilty themselves, then they had been misused and deceived. Leaving aside these different political and moral considerations and levels of consciousness, the war confronted military leaders with new concepts of warfare, as did the Korean and Vietnam wars. The rules of warfare had to be reconsidered and developed accordingly. Above all, the political responsibility and moral justification for the further use of military force in achieving political aims had to be re-assessed. The main developments were these:

— the introduction of new weapons systems opened up the possibility of operations involving several continents. When the interests of the great powers were at stake and they became involved in a war, territorial fighting took on a worldwide dimension. In the Second World War, more than seventy states were drawn in, totalling approximately 80 per cent of the world's population;

— the difference between the front line and the hinterland became even less clearly defined. Civilian populations have been severely hit by air warfare in all wars since 1939. During the Second World War, irregular armed forces and militia groups took part in the fighting to an unknown extent in the Soviet Union, Yugoslavia, France and Italy. Since 1945, the same thing has been happening in Asia and Africa;

— the effects of weapons of mass destruction as well as the growing ideological component of war, as shown in the experience of Hiroshima, increased its destructive character and promoted brutal behaviour and combat patterns which adhered to neither

[13]

legal nor ethical rules. Again, it was the civilian population which suffered most. Of Poland's 6 million dead in the Second World War, 75 per cent were civilians;

— while the Second World War continued, its character changed. The coalition had to solve new political, economic and organizational problems, particularly those of military leadership.

The new dimensions of war may have alarmed the analysts. Our generation of officers, however, was also deeply affected by the course and outcome of the Nuremberg Trials, conducted by an international military tribunal against leading representatives of the former *Wehrmacht*. Generals were put on trial not, as is often assumed, because of their leading positions in an army that had lost the war; they were charged because they had allowed their army to be used by the dictatorship for its criminal purposes. The army had become the instrument which was to carry out Hitler's plan for conquering the world. Every soldier with a sense of responsibility now had to ask himself how such an abuse of military power could be prevented in the future. From this time forward everybody, no matter in which country, deciding to follow a military career, had to face this question. The founding of the United Nations in 1945 gave rise to fresh hopes when it proclaimed that the nations it represented were resolved to 'free future generations from the scourge of war'.[7] The UN Charter places all members under the obligation to settle 'their international conflicts by peaceful means'. The wartime generation of soldiers could thus find fresh hope that their military duty would no longer lead inevitably to war but would serve solely to defend their country and its sovereignty. The postwar period, however, developed differently.

The former British Prime Minister Winston Churchill's anti-Soviet Fulton Speech on 5 May 1946 encouraged those who had not learned their lesson from the past. It disappointed the democratically minded anti-Fascist officers of the former allies against Hitler and it alarmed the peoples who had suffered so much in the war. Later it transpired that — as early as May 1945 — Churchill had ordered the commanders of the British armed forces to collect and store all captured German weaponry for reissue to German soldiers in case of a war with the Soviet Union.[8] Was it just the feeling of victory that made Britain believe it could solve all its problems by military force? Day-to-day politics would soon have corrected this misconception. The effects of the atom bombs on Hiroshima and Nagasaki were worse than anything that could have been imagined and they gave at least an intimation of the potential effects of a possible future nuclear war. But the opposite happened; Churchill's ideas were having an effect. Strategic theories in the USA blossomed into something like a nuclear cult. In 1945, the US Joint Committee of War Planning, in Directive No. 432D, recommended that 196 atom bombs should be held available as a preventive nuclear attack capability for use against the Soviet Union. The Pentagon's Drop-Shot Plan of 1949 demanded 300 atom bombs for a preventive attack. The nuclear hysteria increased in proportion to the growing output of atomic warheads by the US armament industry. By the end of the 1950s there was a certain sobering, when the Soviet Union began to break the USA's nuclear monopoly by developing its own strike capability. The fact that a nuclear conflict did not occur then must not blind people to the possibilities of one in the future.

We have witnessed numerous instances where political aims have been achieved by use of direct or indirect military force. Acting from a position of strength seems to be the present American President's basis for arms negotiations with the Soviet Union. How else can one interpret his insistence that he is willing to negotiate only on a basis of military superiority? Does it not gainsay the lessons learned from the Second World War when his Secretary of State and the Secretary General of NATO advance the view that disagreements with the Arab countries over their oil-exporting policies could be resolved, if necessary, by military intervention? This they call 'an expression of the sense of responsibility' on the part of NATO countries. Is it responsible for leading military representatives of NATO to espouse the claim that wars do not stand in the way of humanity's progress because 'advances in all areas of science and technology, including nuclear energy and space research, stem from the fruits of war'?[9] Even if in the past war has at times provided the stimulus for technological developments, its negative consequences have always been much more serious. In the nuclear age, this line of thought must be given no leeway. The situation is alarming enough when one considers that the idea that there can be 'victory in nuclear war' is put forward in the US by commentators such as Richard Pipes, Colin S. Gray and Keith Payne. The danger threatening us is grave enough without such war scenarios, which verge on the insane. The arms race has led to destructive capability on such a large scale that supervision, checking and accident-free maintenance are becoming increasingly more complicated. Thirty-two accidents with American nuclear weapons were registered between 1950 and 1980.[10] There is a growing danger that a nuclear inferno could start accidentally.

More and more influential people in politics, science and the arts are recognizing the high risks involved. Richard Nixon, the former President of the USA, outlined his approach towards an agreement with the Soviet Union when he said that in the nuclear age the two most important rival powers have to compete with each other with means other than those of war.[11] Despite this warning, nuclear war has become the dominant feature of American military planning and determines the plans evolved by NATO's senior commanders. While we, as former soldiers of the Alliance, may have a particular responsibility for commenting on war and the arms race, it is the general public in every country who must make their politicians face up to the dangers and ensure that events are kept under control. If we are to survive, we can no longer allow a politico-military strategy and the interests of the armaments industry to take precedence over the interests of humanity.

Obedience and conscience — military ethics in the Nuclear Age

Since we disagree with the nuclear arms race and with the use of heavily-armed forces in settling political controversies, the question arises as to how we combine this attitude with the ethics of the military profession.

Our lives were governed by a set of military values — loyalty, service, obedience, courage, comradeship and example. In recent years there have been some additions: love of peace, humanity, responsibility and conscience. These virtues are often included in military oaths, in military laws and in the educational principles for armed forces and they are quite similar in countries which have differing political structures. Whether it is a monarchy or a republic, a democratic or autocratic governmental system, an officer's code of honour is based on the same principles. However, the fact that the same ethical and moral values for soldiers are universally accepted does not mean that they are universally interpreted. In different societies, different criteria can apply, as provided for by foreign and domestic policy. Thus, the canon of military virtues will differ in different countries, with senior officers, whose views have been shaped by tradition, interpreting those military virtues according to their tenets and passing them on to their subordinates. It is our conviction that it is time for these values to be re-asserted in a form which faces up to the new concepts of war.

The armies in the American War of Independence in 1776 were recruited from small farmers, merchants and ordinary citizens. In their battle for independence from English colonial rule they displayed patriotism, courage and valour. They were dedicated and willing to make sacrifices in order to serve their revolutionary ideals. None of the regular armies of the big European powers was strong enough to resist Napoleon's attacks so long as his officers and men were united in the common cause of loyalty towards the Revolutionary and republican values of liberty. When, however, Napoleon turned to a war policy of oppressing other peoples and conquering foreign territories, the ethical and moral motivation of his soldiers dwindled and the tables were turned. Courage, valour and obedience became the values of the united armies of Prussia, Russia, Saxony and other European states in their war of liberation from French domination. The British Royal Air Force pilots of the 1940 Battle of Britain fought with the same courage, dedication and patriotism as did the Russian defenders of Stalingrad in 1943. They were impelled by the knowledge that the fate of their countries depended on how they performed in battle. All the virtues of a soldier's life were put to the test and the result was often true heroism.

Studies in military history too often fail to consider the soldier's motivations. Negative societal factors, especially the abuse of military virtues, are seldom critically assessed; nor are the criminal results condemned. Do not writers of official war histories still try to pass over German crimes in the Second World War and the brutal war waged by the United States in Vietnam? From many possible examples, we cite that of General Smedley D. Butler, formerly commander of the US Marines, who wrote that he had helped, in 1914, to make Mexico 'safe' for American oil interests; he had assisted in the 'cleaning-up' of Cuba and Haiti so that the 'guys' of the National City Bank could collect their profits undisturbed and he had 'cleaned up' Nicaragua for the banking house of Brown Brothers. In 1916 he made 'a clean sweep' in the Dominican Republic for American sugar interests and in 1930 he put Honduras 'in order' for US fruit concerns.[12] The abuse of the military has rarely been so openly admitted.

In our military careers we also faced events, tasks and situations which moved us to question how much we could demand of our officers and men. What was still consistent with international law and when did one become an accessory to a war crime? Often we had to write operation orders which required our subordinates to perform acts of courage in the highest military tradition. Military values do not flourish in predatory wars. On the contrary, they encourage a mercenary mentality which sees war as an escape from civilization and as providing an opportunity to get rich. These and other questions concerning the ethics and the conscience of the soldier were easy to answer as long as one believed that the military aims were justifiable. Operations without prospects of victory or those which violate international law, however, lead to a degeneration of military virtues.

Apart from the war objective and the military mission, there is another factor that plays an important role in developing and maintaining military virtues; it is the personal example set by the military leader. His capacity to lead is determined by the following traditional patterns of behaviour:

— with few exceptions, an élitist consciousness of rank prevails among the officers. Their conduct towards non-commissioned officers and men is often arrogant and is meant to maintain a distance. Part of the reason for this is the preference for officer cadets from the wealthy classes, with their advantageous social and educational backgrounds. For example, between 1870 and 1959, 90 per cent of British officers were sons of the land-owners or of the wealthy middle class. Among German officers the comparative rate was 91 per cent for the period between 1865 and 1930.[13] Slight structural changes that have taken place in recent years have not significantly altered the situation;

— state constitutions guarantee equal rights for all citizens and equal opportunities in military service. It is the case, however, that nationalist, racist and religious prejudices and interests can influence the attitudes of officers and men of the armed forces. Conflict and discrimination between black and white servicemen, between Christian and Jewish soldiers or Catholic and Protestant officers, do occur and do impair the military and the moral standards of the armed forces;

— in armies where personality cults are built around commanders and where there is an over-emphasis on the rules of military order, the officer corps can easily become a stronghold for right-wing radical and anti-democratic political attitudes and groups;

[18]

— the rapid development of the industrial–military complex has led to the introduction of large quantities of sophisticated weapons and equipment. The number of highly-trained technocrats coming into the armed services has resulted in a marked technocratic influence which often prevails over the social and political considerations which apply and the effects which modern weapon systems will have in the event of war;

— the élitist character of the officer corps has been only slightly modified. It often breeds intolerance towards people with other views, particularly toward pacifists and opponents of armament.

Although we were not a party to these patterns of behaviour and endeavoured not to be touched by them, we still had to face them. Conflicts of conscience arose and it required a great deal of resolve and heart-searching to overcome some of our reservations. For some of us the turning point was the Second World War; for others it was the nuclear arms race.

Most of our considerations sooner or later raised questions concerning the limits of the soldier's oath and its demand for obedience to the supreme political and military command. What precisely are the limits to which political leaders can stretch their demand for obedience and what are the limits of a soldier's duty to obey? During the Second World War, for example, French generals and officers had reached the position of making personal decisions about these limits by the summer of 1940. Asked when he had made the most important decision of his career, Admiral Antoine Sanguinetti replied:

> In the course of the war we had to decide whether we were going to obey the French State of Marshal Petain who collaborated with Hitler or to disobey and join the Resistance against the Nazi system. This is the great perception which General de Gaulle taught the military men of my generation: the army always has to serve the nation — without any reservations. That is part of our constitution. Therefore, the army may even turn against the state when the state betrays the higher interests or the moral foundations of the nation.[14]

Officers of the Allied forces observed with great respect that patriotic German officers risked their lives by courageously turning against Hitler's tyranny. They disobeyed the system because they did not want to become accessories to the crimes committed against the peoples of Europe. The majority of German officers were at first shocked and

[19]

hesitant and this enabled Hitler's executioners to seize the opportunity and brutally wipe out the opposition. However, a great many officers were inspired by the patriots of 20 July 1944 and began to reconsider their position. Going beyond their military task, they assessed the inner state of the nation and the war objectives of the Fascist state;

— they thought of the ways of saving Germany from the catastrophe into which the Fascists were driving it;
— they recollected the humanist traditions of the military virtues which, in accordance with the provisions of international law, forbid mass murder, the taking of hostages and brutality against non-combatants and civilians;
— simultaneously, although still hesitantly, they began to criticise the Fascist dictatorship;
— the conviction grew that the generals' and officers' duty of obedience was inconsistent with the crimes of the Fascist state leaders. They no longer felt bound by their soldier's oath.

Nevertheless, the majority of German officers and generals remained passive. Even the lost war and the sentences passed at the Nuremberg Trials did not have a lasting effect. Many of them still clung to their discredited attitudes and behaviour. They blamed their 'bad luck' on unfavourable circumstances and began to make up for their 'lost victories' in new sand-table exercises.

Meanwhile, the International Military Court had passed sentences and drawn up statutes which placed upon soldiers the ethical and moral obligations never again to tolerate such blind obedience. Soldiers were to oppose any preparations that might lead to another war, to refrain from the corruption of the younger generation and the disparagement of people with different opinions. They were required to respect national and international laws as well as racial, religious, and political affiliations.

Unfortunately, however, we were to observe that the lessons of the Second World War, and the critical ideas which had evolved at that time, were soon forgotten. People who had begun to think critically, left the army. Many had reached retiring age but this was not the sole reason for leaving. During the McCarthy era in the United States, a number of officers were discharged because they had been thoroughly convinced of the Allies' democratic and anti-Fascist war aims and were not willing to turn against yesterday's Russian companions-in-arms. Young officers who had no experience of war themselves joined the armed forces. Influential groups used the mass media to spread the idea of a new menace and revitalized the old attitudes for psychological purposes. With the beginning of the nuclear arms race, the use of the media to influence people's minds reached tremendous proportions. Popular fears of a nuclear war were ruthlessly exploited to get new armament legislation passed.

Citizens' initiatives and peace initiative groups offered resistance. Military leaders were called upon to declare their true positions and, whatever they said for or against, nuclear armament was more than just the factual assessment of a military expert. It also related to the relationship between the political task of the armed forces and the limits of military obedience in the nuclear age. The late Lord Louis Mountbatten, former Admiral and Chief of the British Defence Staff, declared: 'I can honestly state that the nuclear arms race serves no military purpose at all. With nuclear weapons you cannot wage a war'.[15] Lord Mountbatten's appeal to all reponsible political and military leaders to 'pull the emergency brake' and to face their responsibilities, has met with the approval of more and more prominent people. It is significant that those who voice their protest against the nuclear arms race most determinedly come from the ranks of the military experts with the greatest knowledge of nuclear weapons and their effects. One of them is Admiral Rickover, the founder of the American strategic submarine fleet; another is General Pasti, former Deputy Superior Commander responsible for nuclear questions at Supreme Headquarters Allied Powers Europe (SHAPE). Admiral Sanguinetti describes his experiences with the destructive power of nuclear weapons:

A man who has witnessed a nuclear explosion asks no further questions but changes his thinking habits radically. He realizes, once and for all, that he is no longer dealing with explosives, not even in massive or gigantic dosages. One is overawed in the face of a horrible and inconceivable catastrophe that has been triggered by man but cannot be controlled by him. It does not matter which side you are on, you will never use the same arguments you did before. I personally witnessed six nuclear explosions.[16]

A military leader who understands the implications of a nuclear war will be aware of his new and special responsibility. He cannot restrict himself to planning and to advising his Government on the most effective use of weapons in war. He must apply his special knowledge to advising his Government and other relevant bodies on how to prevent

[21]

the use of nuclear weapons. Most especially, those high-ranking military leaders who help to develop their countries' defence strategies should look for ways of preventing conflicts and work for nuclear disarmament. If politicians hesitate to consider disarmament, they should be warned and, should they not listen, the military has a responsibility to warn the general public.

Not every government likes their military leaders to assume such moral conscientiousness. Some governments even use drastic measures to silence the warning officers. The French President Giscard d'Estaing hurriedly discharged Generals de Bollardière and Binoche and Admiral Sanguinetti when they publicly criticised France's and NATO's nuclear policy. But the danger of an atomic war sets limits to military obedience. The soldier should obey first and foremost the human right to live in peace. If his nation and his people are endangered he should do everything to save them and, if necessary, speak out against military aims and plans that may violate this basic right. There are officers who would gladly do so and who would reject preparations for nuclear war but they are torn between conscience on the one hand and legal restrictions on the other. In many countries the construction and national defence legislation deny professional soldiers this right. Other states, like France and West Germany, offer the legal right of disobedience if an order violates human dignity or international law but, in practice, it is often a different matter.

The pertinent clauses of international laws are still insufficiently known. The International Military Court at Nuremberg stated that an individual is not obliged to obey national laws and regulations if they are of a criminal nature or instigate crimes. The United Nations has repeatedly concerned itself with the definition of terms such as 'aggression' and 'war crime'. It has also endeavoured to define preparations for nuclear war in terms of international law. In 1961, the UN General Assembly passed a Declaration on the Prohibition of the Use of Nuclear and Thermo-nuclear Weapons, based on The Hague Land Warfare Convention (1899/1907) and on other international treaties and conventions. Because of its importance to all opponents of nuclear war, we should like to quote parts of the Declaration:

(a) the use of nuclear and thermo-nuclear weapons is contrary to the spirit, letter and aims of the United Nations and, as such, a direct violation of the Charter of the United Nations;
(b) the use of nuclear and thermo-nuclear weapons would exceed

lead us to share the views of the American Catholic bishops who stated in their Pastoral Letter that they saw nuclear war as threatening the existence of this planet. Formerly, one of the primary ethical aims of the church had been to prevent war and — when it happened — to try to limit its consequences. Today the possibilities of limiting a nuclear war are politically and morally extremely few; the church must therefore share with the medical profession the moral duty to strive for the prevention of war.[18] We adhere to the Christian tradition and understand the divine peace commandment as a pillar of the Christian faith. We also interpret it as an order to oppose the threat of nuclear war. It is, of course, deplorable that numerous European religious institutions have so far not taken a firm stand on the nuclear arms race since they believe that decisions about war and peace belong exclusively to the political sphere. This situation is used by conservative clerical groups as an excuse to propagate their endorsement of nuclear armament. Leading West German theologians have pronounced that the use of nuclear weapons 'does not necessarily contradict ethical norms and is not in every case a sin'. One of them went further, declaring: 'Those who talk about the atom bomb in the name of the Gospel cannot overlook the fact that the atom bomb is a means of punishment in the hands of God'.[19] Unlike the American bishops, this pious man obviously did not know what he was talking about and probably had no idea of the destructive potential of nuclear technology. Knowing that Christian opponents to nuclear war act in accordance with deeply-held religious beliefs and only after a thorough examination of their consciences, conservative clerical groups proclaim that 'conscience may be led astray'.[20] But why should it be those who have taken the Christian peace commandment seriously and done nobody any harm who have been led astray? A mis-led conscience could sooner be suspected in those who offer their blessings to the preparation and waging of war. Their conduct is reminiscent of the sorts of error found in history. A Catholic field hymn-book of 1942 contains the prayer. 'Especially bless our Führer and Supreme Commander in all of his missions'. Endorsing nuclear weapons may, however, have far graver consequences than the blessing of Hitler's aggressiveness. The Suffragan Bishop of Rotterdam's diocese criticized the Christian peace movement for its allegedly total intolerance. But a man who supports the deployment of nuclear weapons on Dutch soil can hardly claim to be tolerant of the Dutch Christian's will to stay alive. Deterrence and mass destruction

[24]

have no place in Christian belief. They do not provide Christian answers to the contradictions and conflicts in our world. From a Christian point of view, we can assess the arms race only as the expression of a deep cultural crisis in which the tendency towards brutal self-assertion and exaggeration of military power will lead to a cult of violence that is incompatible with our humility towards God. The Bible offers many examples of determined opposition to evil and to those who disregard humanity's wish to continue living. The Gospels of St Matthew and St John refer to Jesus in the following words: 'And [he] said unto them, It is written, My house shall be called the house of prayer; but ye have made it a den of thieves. . . . And when he had made a scourge of small cords, he drove them all out of the temple, . . '. Today, it is those favouring the arms race who risk turning the globe into a 'nuclear den of cut-throats'. The US bishops' Pastoral Letter describes this as a situation that 'has to be changed, no matter how long and troublesome the task may be'. The Christian groups with the peace movement are devoting themselves to this task. While at first we reacted in a typical and traditional manner towards the peace movement, borne of a deep-rooted suspicion of its motives, this opinion has changed and we have come to be accepted and welcomed as fellow-workers. As a result, new perspectives have opened up in our thinking and have led us to develop new perceptions of the role of the military in politics.

Through the process of thinking through new concepts of war and peace, we have been exposed to the comprehensive character of the peace movement and the broad spectrum of its activities, including the involvement of physicians, churchmen, scientists, lawyers and other professional and community groups. While we have a personal and mature knowledge of war and understand better the technicalities of military fighting with nuclear weapons, it is the members of the peace movement who have emphasized more resolutely the dangers inherent in the exploitation of the nuclear arms race. It has been a new and novel experience for us to see people with different social backgrounds and political views united in a common desire for peace and willing to make personal sacrifices to save mankind from a nuclear catastrophe.

In view of the growing danger to our civilization, we are all responsible for stopping the arms race. If military men and people from all walks of life combine their ideas and work together, we may still be able to prevent the holocaust. The Generals' Group for Peace and Disarmament has devoted itself to this ideal because we see military

[25]

service first and foremost as serving peace. We have publicized our views in numerous statements, initiatives, speeches, and articles. Now, we believe, the time is ripe to present a summary of our political point of view. In spite of our individual political, ethical and religious views, we are agreed on the following basic principles which will be outlined in greater detail in the following chapters:

— in our age of weapons of mass destruction, war is no longer a feasible instrument of politics. The resolution of conflicts in East–West relations can only be achieved by peaceful means;

— the arms race endangers peace. It imposes an unendurable economic and financial burden on national economies and devours the world's dwindling natural resources;

— a policy of security does not require nuclear weapons. The nuclear powers should renounce the first use of nuclear weapons, withdraw them from the territories of non-nuclear countries and seriously negotiate armament control, especially nuclear disarmament;

— we advocate a national defence which concentrates on the strategic principles and military structures of conventional, non-offensive armament and is therefore not suitable for threatening and attacking neighbouring states;

— the long-term aim is to overcome delimitation and confrontation between the military blocs but, firstly, they will have to limit their policies and strategies to defensive objectives. They must develop the ability to resolve conflicts and manage crises with peaceful means;

— we plead for the strengthening of national independence and sovereignty of all states. We advocate the establishment of friendly relations with the Warsaw Pact countries;

— we advocate positive and constructive initiatives in the field of confidence building through greater and more frequent physical contacts at all levels of government, including the military.

The Reagan Administration's Confrontation Policy Increases The Threat of War

Back to the Cold War?

With deep concern, we watched US policy beginning to change in the second half of the 1970s. The change was particularly noticeable in the deterioration of Soviet–US relations which are of paramount importance to East–West relations and world politics.

President Nixon and his Secretary of State Henry Kissinger had based their foreign policy on the clear assumption that the two super-powers were forced to coexist and had to solve their conflicts peacefully. They realized that the Soviets had achieved strategic parity and recognized that more weapons did not mean more security but, on the contrary, only impeded the resolution of political conflicts. At the same time, the US government was under increasing pressure to end the Vietnam war. The Soviet bloc, facing both external and internal problems, such as the growing Chinese threat, economic difficulties and increasing pressure for reform in some of its satellite states (Czechoslovakia, Poland), was becoming increasingly vulnerable to threats to its security other than those of a military kind. What followed was an exercise in pragmatism which accepted the realities of the situation and made possible the SALT negotiations and the Helsinki Conference. This policy approach was widely endorsed by the European countries and provided the framework within which negotiations with the Soviet Union were able to begin.

Such policies of 'appeasement' are always likely to meet with strong resistance in the USA, especially from representatives of the

[27]

military–industrial complex to whose pressure Presidents Nixon, Ford and Carter frequently yielded. Critics argued that the USSR could not be regarded as an equal in super-power terms, with whom binding agreements could be concluded. They saw the USSR as a Communist, and therefore intrinsically hostile, state that was aggressively trying to expand its empire and impose its political culture on the rest of the world. As the Nixon Administration lost credibility because of Watergate, the opponents of détente regained strength. In 1974 they blocked the trade agreement with the Soviet Union (Jackson–Vanik amendment) in order to put pressure on Soviet emigration policy. Nevertheless, the Helsinki Agreement was signed and small advances were achieved on the level of cultural exchange. But the Pentagon's resistance to détente was insurmountable and in 1975 a campaign of hostility toward the Soviet Union was mounted. The Carter Administration's human rights campaign — a disputed issue in Europe — was intended to put further pressure on the Soviets while at the same time the arms race was stepped up. Simultaneously with these moves by the United States, the character of her relationship with her European allies changed from one of partnership to one close to subservience on the latters' part. The changed priorities of US foreign policy reached their climax with President Reagan's strategy of 'direct confrontation with the USSR'.

Thus the line pursued in the 1970s had clearly been abandoned. At that time, conceding the Soviets' strategic parity, American and West European policy had been working towards stabilizing the military balance by agreements and treaties with the long-term aim of a reduction in arms. Military conflicts were regarded as fundamentally dangerous and only justifiable, if at all, in peripheral regions of the Third World. The United States had hesitated before deciding to participate in the Helsinki Conference but it finally recognized the territorial and political status quo in Europe which had evolved after the Second World War. This was the basis of positive developments in economic and cultural relations between East and West. There was also a promising trend towards more trust in international relations and, consequently, towards improved East–West cooperation in many fields, including military issues.

At the end of the 1970s, the United States executed a sharp reversal of policy by refusing to ratify the SALT II agreement which up to that time had been acceptable and could still have been signed in 1979. Whatever were the reasons for the rejection at the time, it is certain that the shifts of political power in the USA played a major part. Today we know that the change was not a chance development. The important posts in the Reagan Administration are held by people from institutions and groups known to be anti-détente, such as the Committee on the Present Danger, the Heritage Foundation, the American Enterprise Institute and the Center for Strategic and International Studies at Georgetown University, Washington. It is deplorable that, as a result of the action taken, the national interests of the West European States were not only ignored but consequently threatened.

The central argument of the Reagan Administration's strategic thinking is that the United States should plan to defeat the Soviet Union and to do so at a cost that would not prohibit US recovery. This new concept was outlined in an article by Colin S. Gray and Keith Payne, published in *Foreign Policy* in the summer of 1980. It was for Washington to identify their war aims which, in the last resort, would consider the destruction of Soviet political authority and the emergence of a postwar world order compatible with Western values.[1] People could hardly believe what they heard when President Reagan outlined his views. It was passed off as mere election propaganda when he stated: 'We are going to strive for increasing defense budgets sufficient to achieve a position of military superiority'.[2] These words, however, were followed by action which allowed the shape of the new policy to become apparent — the notion of approximate strategic parity was replaced by the aim of military superiority; not only peripheral conflicts were to be won but the Soviet Union itself was to be conquered militarily and politically. Economic sanctions were applied and the decisions of the European Security Conference were disregarded. The postwar political and territorial alignment in Europe was queried by President Reagan, who said in London that Poland should not be counted as a member of the Communist bloc. A policy now emerged which tended towards the containment of détente through an escalation of conflict, replacing the previous policy of the containment of conflict through a strengthening of détente. Russian intervention in Cambodia, Afghanistan and Poland provided adequate pretexts for abandoning détente, though there may have been an ulterior motive in wishing to distract attention from the USA's use of defoliants and other chemical agents in Vietnam, to obscure its pro-Israeli policies and its support of the totalitarian regimes of Latin America.

[29]

Obviously, the military play a decisive role in this policy of confrontation. If confrontations are to be won, military superiority must be gained — a fact which both Presidents Carter and Reagan have demonstrated by a succession of armament programmes aimed at achieving this objective. In May 1978, the NATO Conference adopted a Long Term Defense Programme (LTDP) designed to guarantee an annual increase of 3 per cent in arms expenditure and a modernization of all components of NATO's armed forces by 1993.

The first nuclear submarine of the *Ohio* class was launched in April 1979 and in June President Carter ordered the development of a new intercontinental ballistic missile system, the MX. In December of the same year the Special Session of Foreign and Defence Ministers at Brussels decided to deploy 572 American intermediate range nuclear systems in Western Europe from 1983 on. Their range and accuracy of aim provide a first strike capacity against the USSR from European soil.

In his State of the Union Message of January 1980, President Carter announced a five-year armament plan that provided for a further development in US strategic nuclear potential, an improvement and modernization of the armed forces and for the fast build-up of 'strategic strike forces' intended to further strengthen a world-wide military presence. In July 1980, President Carter's Directive 59 extended the operational principles of nuclear warfare to include a first strike capability against strategic targets in the USSR. Since then there have been other adjustments to the theory of warfare. President Reagan's Defense Directives 1984–88, parts of which have been leaked, contain provisions for a quantitative and qualitative increase in strategic nuclear arms potential with the objective of 'decapitating' the Soviet Union, for improving conventional warfare capabilities in theatres of war all over the world, as well as for the improvement of special operations capabilities. It also contains measures to step up psychological, economic and technological warfare.

Thus, Gray's 'victory is possible' theory has been turned into a concrete programme which affects all levels of politics. It is designed to ensure the success of the 'crusade against Communism' outlined in President Reagan's speech to the British Parliament on 8 June 1982. In this speech, Reagan announced:

What I am describing now is a plan and a hope for the long term, the march of freedom and democracy which will leave Marxism–Leninism on the ashheap of history as it has left other tyrannies which stifle the freedom and muzzle the self-expression of the people. That is why we must continue our efforts to strengthen NATO even as we move forward with our zero option initiative in the negotiations on intermediate-range forces and our proposal for a one-third reduction in strategic ballistic missile warheads. Our military strength is a prerequisite to peace but let it be clear that we maintain this strength in the hope it will never be used. For the ultimate determinant in the struggle now going on for the world will not be bombs and rockets but a test of wills and ideas, a trial of spiritual resolve, the values we hold, the beliefs we cherish, the ideals to which we are dedicated.[3]

There are signs of criticism and uneasiness among the European allies but the politicians and bodies responsible for military matters continue to increase military expenditure. The money is being used to finance qualitatively new weapon systems which are to change the military balance between East and West in favour of the West. One may safely assume that this will prove to be an illusion but by then billions will have been squandered and possible chances for an arms reduction and for a limitation of military confrontation will have been lost.

This policy is by no means accepted uncritically, even in the USA. As early as 6 July 1981, George W. Ball, former Under Secretary of State and head of the American UN delegation, wrote in the *Washington Post*: 'Such an attitude is not a policy but an obsession.... If our current blindly reckless course worries our European friends, it should worry us fully as much. The Administration seems bent on persuading the Soviet Union that it foresees an unlimited arms race and has lost interest in peaceful working relations'.

George F. Kennan also realized the dangers of a policy of confrontation. As 'Mr X', Kennan had drafted the policy of political 'containment' towards the Soviet Union. Having held the important post of US Ambassador in Moscow and being one of the Americans best informed on the subject of Soviet policy, since an early stage he has realized the folly of a confrontation policy. As early as 28 August 1981, he wrote in the West German weekly *Die Zeit* that the reasons for the present danger to human life are to be found 'in the terrible militarization of thinking . . . , in the kind of obsession which compels all who have fallen prey to it to direct their entire attention to the hopeless eventualities of a military conflict and, at the same time, to ignore the hopeful chances of talking to each other to achieve a

[31]

balance'. But how can such words be effective when they are pitted against the material interests of those industries making substantial profits out of the present situation? On 5 August 1981, Secretary of Defense Caspar Weinberger stated in the *Washington Post* that the US defence industry ought to be prepared 'to skim off half of the gross national product in case of emergency'.

We should like to consider some further points contained in Defense Directives 1984–88, especially insofar as they have already become practical policy. The translation of the theory into practice happens very quickly. None of the former US Administrations have implemented anti-détente policies as determinedly, as quickly and as irresponsibly as the present one. The policy of increased armament expenditure has naturally had an effect on arms limitation and disarmament negotiations. In July 1981 the Reagan Administration's First Secretary of State, Alexander Haig, pointed out in a keynote address that we have learnt by experience that armament control can be only one element within the structure of defence and foreign policy; that it cannot be the key political element in or the decisive barometer of American-Soviet relations; that armament control should complement military strategy and that if the West would make their defence programmes dependent on progress in armament control then the Soviets would see no reason to negotiate fair agreements. In the vital relationship between armaments and their control the cart must not come before the horse![4]

Thus arms will continue to be piled up, no matter what happens at the negotiating table. According to this view, only from a position of strength can the US force the Soviet Union to the negotiating table — there to extort unilateral advantages. In the early days of disarmament efforts, this view has prevented any progress in negotiations. SALT became possible only after it had been abandoned.

This approach explains why the Reagan Administration was willing to return to the conference table only after public opinion and the peace movement in the United States began to exert increased pressure. In the same speech, Haig said that 'the international conduct of the Soviet Union has a direct bearing on the chances of success in arms control'.[5] And Eugene Rostow, former Chief of the Arms Control and Disarmament Agency (ACDA), later admitted that the President had instructed him to the effect that such a package deal could not be allowed 'to be merely a temporary and isolated Soviet step'.[6]

The US as well as other Western countries have been severely hit by

[32]

the economic crisis. At the end of January 1983, there were 32 million official 'poor' in the US, 13 million unemployed, 2 million homeless and 11 million Americans who had lost their right to health insurance. Nowadays, there are people who go hungry in the richest country in the world and the infant mortality rate is rising. The Administration would seem to disregard the real needs of these people. It ignores the economic interests of those groups within industry whose survival in a time of depression depends upon East–West trade. Apart from a few cosmetic alterations, there is no sign of a limitation in the armament programme. Economic relations with East European countries are being used to exert pressure in order to exacerbate their economic crises, weaken their alliance and to compel conduct amenable to US policy. There should be no trade without political conditions, the National Security Council's former expert on Soviet affairs, Richard Pipes, announced bluntly.[7] Alexander Haig had already stated that the Soviet leaders would have to learn that there could be no full and normal economic relations as long as they were not willing to respect the rules of international conduct.[8] This is why the American Government orderd a halt to US firms' deliveries for the Soviet–West European natural gas pipeline project which had been guaranteed by a complex network of agreements. European subsidiaries were put under pressure and the sovereignty of European states was simply ignored. West European industry was expected to implement American dictates. Regardless of the fact that trade with the East is more important for Europe than for the United States, Europe was expected to put the American trade embargo into effect. In direct contrast, President Reagan bowed to the interests of his own farmers and revoked the grain embargo.

Where credits have been granted to Communist countries at all, they have been granted selectively. Myer Rashish, Under Secretary of State for Economic Affairs, explained that they too should serve the furtherance of evolutionary change, of an increasing emphasis on the interests of individual nations and of a greater consideration for the rights of individual citizens by Eastern-bloc governments.[9]

The Administration is bringing strong pressure to bear on US industry and its European allies to refrain from transferring technology to Eastern Europe through a set of restrictive practices called for by the NATO coordinating committee, COCOM. However, history teaches us that embargoes more often than not fail to achieve their purpose. Those against the Soviet Union have not prevented or curtailed its production and deployment of conventional and nuclear arms; nor the Soviet Union's conquest of space. They did not change Soviet emigration policy, or Soviet policy towards Poland or Afghanistan. Instead, they disturbed international relations, impeded international trade and led to disputes with the allies, not to mention the heightening of tension created in relations with the opposite side. That is a high price to pay for an essentially ineffective measure.

Trade has always been a link between peoples and countries. It is absurd to use it to disturb peaceful relations and to frustrate the wishes of those who desire to live and work in peace. The Reagan Administration will find it difficult to persuade the American people and those of the Western nations that this policy is in their best interests unless it succeeds in convincing them that the Soviets represent a terrifying threat; an artificially-contrived image that has been a part of the present Administration propaganda since it was elected.

Since the London speech in which President Reagan announced his 'crusade against Communism', steps have been taken to put these ideas into practice. In October 1982, the US State Department held a Conference on the Democratization of Communist Countries, with participants ranging from government representatives, journalists, and professors to representatives of emigrants' organizations and trades unions. Secretary of State Schultz told the Conference that the West has a moral duty to support democratic political movements everywhere in the world. The US Government would not ignore those individuals and groups in Communist countries who are striving for peaceful change. He went on to say that 'we have a responsibility to respond to their cries for help, morally and strategically'.[10]

This amounts to a comprehensive programme of interference in other countries' internal affairs and of changing domestic political relationships in Communist countries. The simultaneous assurance that there is no intention of creating disorder and that only peaceful change would be supported does not carry much conviction, nor is it particularly novel. At the time of the Hungarian uprising in 1956, the two US Munich-based broadcasting stations, Radio Free Europe and Radio Liberty, were used extensively in support of those opposed to the Hungarian regime, though this was as far as US intervention went. At the Washington Conference, Schultz announced that the two Munich stations were to receive an additional 44 million dollars in 1982. The overall costs of world-wide propaganda broadcasting are calculated to

[34]

be more than 1,000 million dollars. Stations broadcasting abroad are to be modernized and high hopes are held for the future use of satellites.[11]

President Carter's human rights campaign has emerged as something different from its original concept. It is one thing to sympathize with dissidents in Communist countries and to protest against restrictions imposed on them by the authorities but it is a different matter to use them as instruments for changing the political system. Memories of recent events in Poland are still fresh. In view of the Washington Conference, the support of American trades unions for Solidarity in Poland could be seen in a different light. At the height of the Polish crisis, the Munich broadcasting stations immediately increased their broadcasts in Polish, giving detailed instructions to opposition groups. The form in which news was broadcast — repeated at short intervals — allowed these groups to coordinate their activities and helped them to disseminate their information about their underground operations. Used in this way, broadcasting to foreign countries does not facilitate better understanding; instead, it becomes a means of de-stabilization.

Every country has the right to project an image of itself in the way it pleases in its broadcasts to foreign countries. However, it is unacceptable for a broadcasting station to claim to be presenting an alternative mass media programme for other countries; this is precisely the position taken by the US Government's information experts. The practice of telling the media what they should broadcast by, for example, briefing journalists on how they should handle issues such as democracy, disarmament or Communism is particularly disturbing. Campaigns have been initiated with the aim to present views and opinions in a one-sided and prejudiced way. In a free society, we reject this approach since it destroys our highly-valued principle of plurality of views.

In the United States, several groups have been formed to influence public opinion in Western Europe in favour of the planned deployment of US missiles. Security advisor Clark had been appointed chairman of a group which also included Secretary of State Schultz, Secretary of Defense Weinberger, USIA Chief Charles Wick, and the Chairman of the International Development Aid Programme, Peter McPherson. The group's task was to guarantee the 'coherence of foreign policy statements' of various administrative bodies in order to 'neutralize the Soviet peace offensive'. Another group, which includes representatives of the CIA, is led by Peter Dailey, US Ambassador in Ireland. The special target of this group is Western Europe. According to the *Neue Züricher Zeitung*, the aim is to counter the arguments put forward by opponents of the deployment of US intermediate-range missiles, who are being increasingly listened to in Europe. In private life, Dailey is the head of the advertising agency which conducted President Reagan's election campaign in 1980.[12]

The British peace movement, Campaign for Nuclear Disarmament (CND), has already been the target of the group's methods of manipulation. The pressures exerted on those sections of the peace movement which merely make use of their constitutional rights of free speech and political activity are a foretaste of what is awaiting continental European countries now that the missile deployment has taken place. British newspapers reported that more than a dozen organizations hostile to CND were formed within a very short time. They launched their attacks from various quarters, denouncing CND, quite unjustifiably, as an agent of Moscow while rejecting any possibility for an open discussion on the issues raised. Even such a serious paper as *The Times* supported this attack. Officially the groups are independent of political parties but in reality they include influential members of the Conservative Party. The groups include Coalition for Peace Through Security, the Committee for Peace in Freedom, and the British Atlantic Committee. They receive financial support directly from the state budget. Thus, without any objective discussion, state finances are being used to wage a secret psychological war.[13] This is a most disturbing development in the motherland of modern democracy and a form of attack on a political adversary that is unworthy of the European intellectual tradition. These developments show clearly what the results of Reagan's strategies can be in practical terms. They lead to political unrest at home and produce international instability. It is high time such methods were abandoned.

Irresponsible images of the enemy

Anyone going to Washington to discuss the trends of US foreign affairs could not be blamed for thinking that the USA is moving towards a war footing in preparation for the outbreak of war. This is reflected in recent opinion polls in which the majority of American citizens believe that peace is threatened and that war is highly possible. There is a general feeling that only military means can solve political conflicts and that there is no hope of reaching agreement with the Soviets at the negotiating table. It is exactly the mood of the Cold War of the 1950s.

Political communication between the super-powers seems to have broken down completely. The political establishment of the USA is dominated by the view, expressed franky by Richard Pipes, that the Soviet leaders must choose the peaceful transformation of the Communist system in accordance with the Western model, or there will be war.[14] The deployment of Cruise and Pershing II missiles has further aggravated the situation by causing the breaking-off of negotiations. Even alliance partners are experiencing difficulty in understanding each other. We Europeans are having to face up once again to the pseudo alternative of the Cold War period and must make a choice. Our group has made that choice. We believe that US policy is placing at risk the whole structure of civilization, not only in Europe but also in the world. That is why we cannot agree with the present Administration's over-simplified world view that suspects the hand of Moscow behind every evil. Regardless of one's views of the Soviet system, to believe it can be changed from outside is a naïve illusion.

The history of the American presidency shows that each president in turn goes through a process of learning in foreign policy. Although it is always difficult to abandon policies determined by domestic priorities, ultimately every president has developed a foreign policy perspective appropriate to the existing international situation. During his time in office, President Reagan has totally destroyed any confidence which was being established in East–West relations. He himself has shattered any belief in his 'ability to learn'. Experiments take time and today time is a strategic category. Lost time means lost opportunities of securing peace, and instability in Soviet-American relations which are of such vital importance for the world today. That is why more and more Americans are calling for a return to reason. George F. Kennan has repeatedly warned that it is no longer possible to tackle the problems of Soviet-American relations other than in a sober, objectively analytical, consistent, serious and pragmatic fashion. He has also stressed that there is little time left to impress the necessity for such an approach on the American consciousness.[15]

The increased importance of the military factor in US policies has necessarily raised new questions about the military balance of power and about strategic objectives. Above all, it has raised the question of the perceived Soviet military threat. More than ever before, military problems have become a matter of public opinion and of political concern. The literature on this subject is endless. Basically, this is a positive development because it shows that the importance of the problems of war and peace in our age has been recognized. However, certain negative aspects cannot be overlooked.

Technical language which is difficult to understand often obscures even simple issues and the interpretation of complicated military matters requires a high degree of technical knowledge. Wherever this is lacking, there is a potential danger of manipulation. The layman has to differentiate between real knowledge and charlatanism and quite often he is unable to do so. However, we think it is wrong to avoid the difficulties involved in coming to terms with complex military, and military policy, issues. Unless this is done, judgements about who is threatening whom, and which military aims are realistic, can be made only on the basis of conjecture and emotion. The major assumptions on which the policy of confrontation is based may be summarized as follows:

(a) the United States and the other members of NATO are militarily weak; the USSR and its Warsaw Pact allies are militarily strong. The Western alliance increases armaments only according to necessity and is limited by low budgets, whereas the Warsaw Pact continues its excessive armament free of economic restrictions;

(b) the Soviet Union is inherently aggressive and expansionist, as is every other Communist state. Every weakness shown by the West is ruthlessly exploited by the Russians. The Soviet intervention in Afghanistan and Soviet support of Third World liberation movements, whose activities are often described as bordering on terrorism, are cited as proof. The peaceful character of Western armament and behaviour is, by contrast, undisputed and therefore barely requires corroboration;

(c) in principle, Communist politicians' proposals and statements should be viewed with caution and distrust. The breaching of promises and of contract are basic attributes of Soviet foreign policy. Recently William Clark, former head of the US Security Council, contended that 'historically speaking the Soviet Union has given little reason for believing in its willingness to keep its word'.[16]

Thus, a general image is created of the Soviet Union and its allies as evil powers, armed to the teeth and ready for attack if we, the potential victims, should show signs of weakness. If the charge of direct military aggressiveness does not stand up, then it is the Soviet Union's 'exertion

[38]

of military pressure' that obviously threatens us. The basic inference is always the same: the West has no alternative but continually to step up its armament.

The main US analyses of the military challenge are based on comparisons of potentials. By its very existence, the Soviet military potential is considered a challenge and a threat. On the other hand, the Soviet Union has no grounds for considering NATO's Long Term Armament programme as preparations for a first strike capability, nor the concept of 'decapitating blows' as a challenge. Numbers of tanks, aircraft, missiles, ships and divisions, are painstakingly compared. The numerical advantages of the Warsaw Pact, thus proved, are taken to constitute a military challenge. This challenge, in turn, necessitates a demand for higher budgets to modernize and strengthen defence potential. However, this quantitative comparison of existing forces has several methodological shortcomings. It is a method which is neither original nor scientifically accurate but plays on the general public's limited technical knowledge and tries to make up for a lack of proof by a continual re-statement of such suspect statistical data, tailored to suit the purpose. For instance, only those armament systems are selected for comparison where the USSR is known to be numerically superior, while the qualitative comparison, generally in favour of the West, is not stated. Nor are those systems where the USA hold numerical superiority brought into the equation. The best example of this brand of selective counting is in the land-based missiles of the strategic weapon system. Not only are they extremely vulnerable to attack but they represent the largest proportion of the Soviet's nuclear arsenal whereas the USA has concentrated its effort into submarine and aircraft missile systems.

The comparison of forces is usually limited to the consideration of those of the USA and the USSR alone, instead of taking the whole of NATO and the Warsaw Pact into consideration. This makes it possible to disregard the nuclear weapons of Great Britain and France as well as the huge conventional potential of Western European NATO countries, which is much larger than that of the Warsaw Pact states minus the Soviet Union. The latter therefore has to compensate for the gap.

A basic mathematical rule, of only comparing like with like, is violated when the following are compared:
— armaments systems with different qualitative characteristics;
— divisions whose strength in NATO is approximately double that

of divisions in the Warsaw Pact;
— quality of troops, which involves factors like motivation, training, leadership, etc. — areas in which NATO is clearly superior.

Facts and figures are taken out of context. Thus a comparison merely of the number of Soviet and American tanks not only neglects to take into account their quality and the relevant number of anti-tank weapons available, it also ignores the fact that the USSR is a continental power with a long frontier which needs defending at several points, whereas the USA has nothing to fear at its borders, either in the north from Canada or in the south from Mexico. American tanks are needed only for American activities overseas, in Europe, Asia, South America and Africa. In principle, the same is also true of fighters and combat aircraft.

Important categories within the political and economic balance of power which are of great military significance are not taken into account. The member states of NATO:
— have an industrial potential much greater than that of the Warsaw Pact states;
— have nearly twice as many inhabitants;
— have a system of military bases which encircle the Soviet Union and its allies like an iron ring;
— are more advanced in military technology, which in the past has allowed them always to be the first to introduce decisive new elements in armament technology.

It would be wrong, however, to underestimate the Soviet Union's military potential. It is significant and, in some areas, superior to that of the USA or NATO but, when viewed as a whole, there is an approximate balance between the forces of the two alliances. There is as little reason to deny NATO's capability as there is to assume that the Warsaw Pact will stand idly by while the West moves ahead in the arms race. As George Kennan also pointed out, we must bring the potentially disastrous militarization of public debate on East–West relations to an end; we must stop the constant talk about the terrible things we could do to the Russians and they could do to us in an allegedly inevitable war. We must also stop presenting the presumable intentions and military preparations of this potential enemy to the public in an increasingly threatening light. More generally, we must cease from the only too frequent and systematic denigration of another great people and its government — denigration which, if not checked soon, will make war unavoidable in fact by making it appear so.[17]

The retired German General Christian Krause, in an objective analysis of the methodology required to manage a military conflict, concludes that the 'capacity to conduct a war requires much more than just military strength. The response capacity of the side being attacked, and the consequences for one's own side, have to be taken into acount. Account has to be taken of the geo-strategic, economic and other effects that could follow'.

According to the West German Government's White Paper for 1975-6, the population of the NATO countries exceeds that of the Warsaw Pact countries by approximately 200 million. The gross national product of the NATO countries is twice that of the Warsaw Pact countries. Other Western sources report that NATO's conventional armed forces are roughly equal to those of the Warsaw Pact but that NATO have more nuclear warheads. Long-term analysis shows that the members of NATO spend about twice as much on armament as do the Warsaw Pact countries, while it holds a substantial lead in technology. All these comparisons lead to the same conclusion: the resources of NATO are considerably larger than those of the Warsaw Pact, while military potentials are at least equal, giving NATO the edge in conflict management. But the comparison is not yet complete. NATO itself is only one segment of the whole US alliance structure directed against the USSR. In 1979 the USA had almost 100 bi-lateral agreements with other countries, many of them including clauses about military aid, military training, air agreements, logistic support and bases. The US system of alliances covers the whole globe. It encompasses the Pacific as well as the Atlantic and extends to the Indian Ocean and Australasia. All the industrial nations of the non-Communist world, including Japan, are a part of it.

The Western Alliance controls the sea routes and thus effectively controls a large part of the world's natural resources and sources of energy. If the Soviet Union should attack Europe, the risk of world-wide war is very great. That is why Europe cannot be considered in isolation when the Soviet Union's capabilities for warfare are assessed.[18]

A key problem which emerges from the overall global comparison is the relative balance in strategic nuclear weapon systems. The common basis for all assessments is still SALT II because both sides have kept essentially to its guidelines, even though the US refused to ratify it. The agreement can be regarded as a positive step because it provides the starting point for a commonly agreed procedure for assessing the balance of forces. In the SALT II agreement, which was signed in the summer of 1979, both sides settled on the following numbers of strategic delivery systems: USA = 2,283; USSR = 2,504. Here the USA held an advantage in the number of multiple independently targetable re-entry vehicles (MIRVs). However, the agreement set an approximate parity between the super-powers. Prominent US politicians admit that the approximate balance still exists. It is only members of the Reagan Administration who claim that the Soviet Union has superiority. According to the Stockholm International Peace Research Institute (SIPRI), the United States today has 10,154 MIRV warheads at its disposal and the USSR more than 7,078.[19] Even this does not lead Soviet commentators to insist that a change in the strategic balance of forces has taken place. Naturally, the warheads are differently distributed among the various kinds of delivery vehicles in accordance with the different geo-strategic situation of the two super-powers. The US Center for Defense Information supplied the following figures:

	USA	USSR
Land-based intercontinental ballistic missiles (ICBM)	2,147	5,238
Submarine-launched intercontinental ballistic missile (SLBM)	4,960	1,698
Air-launched intercontinental ballistic missiles aboard strategic bombers	2,668	290
Total of strategic nuclear weapons	9,775	7,226

SIPRI points out that the USA has a particular advantage in that about half of its strategic nuclear weapons are deployed on nuclear submarines, which are at present invulnerable, whereas the Soviet Union has deployed only a quarter of its strategic potential in this way. According to SIPRI's figures, the total number of nuclear weapons in East and West, including tactical systems with a relatively short range, is 31,000 for NATO and 20,000 for the Warsaw Pact. In Europe, the United States has more than 6,000 tactical nuclear weapons at her disposal, while the French and British armed forces have approximately 500.[20] It therefore remains a mystery how President Reagan can calculate that the West is inferior in terms of nuclear weapons.

According to Marshal Shulman, former special adviser to the US Department of State:

> The Soviet Union does not have any usable nuclear-military superiority . . . but the scale of destruction of nuclear weapons is so great that the nuclear-military balance is not a delicate one. Even if the disparities in one nuclear category or another were greater than they are, neither side could attack the other without suicidal effect. The fact is that we have a sturdy balance of mutual deterrence.[21]

Moreover, the development of the controversial land-based MX missiles and the submarine-launched Trident II missiles is designed to achieve a strategic advantage for the United States. Both systems are so accurate that they are classified as 'capable of first strike'. This means that in the event of a surprise preventive first strike, they could be used to eliminate Soviet strategic systems and to put civilian as well as military command centres out of action.

The way in which the term 'strategic weapons' has been manipulated is also revealing. In their negotiations on strategic arms limitation, the Americans and the Soviets agreed to classify as 'strategic' those systems which are capable of reaching the territory of the other super-power. The distance between the USA and the Soviet Union (5,500 kilometres) was agreed upon as the criterion by which weapons with a range of 5,500 kilometres were to be judged as strategic; the criterion fails to apply when such weapons are deployed at distances within which shorter-range weapons can be equally effective, since it would be justifiable to designate the latter weapons as strategic.

This needs to be kept in mind in discussions about intermediate-range missiles. In spite of their shorter range, they are clearly strategic systems. This is only partially true of submarine-launched missiles because

— their number has been settled by negotiations and
— at the present time their accuracy does not compare with that of land-based missiles (i.e. they are not 'capable of first strike').

The essential advantages of a forward-based deployment of these shorter-range nuclear weapons for the United States cannot be overlooked:

— officially they are not counted as strategic systems;
— some of them (Pershing II) can use the 'time factor' as a strategic element, meaning that their early warning time is reduced to a

[43]

fraction of that of intercontinental missiles;
— counter strikes against missile sites will not be directed at US territory;
— the precision of the guided missile systems is much greater than that of the strategic weapons so far deployed.

Why should the United States be prepared to forego these weapons? Negotiations so far have shown that it has no intention of doing so.

Since a superiority in strategic armament cannot be established for either side, the question then arises of the balance in conventional forces. Has NATO not improved its combat capabilities and its readiness for action in the past few years? Do we now need to step up armament in order to counter Soviet superiority and to be able to resist any possible attempt by the Kremlin to conquer the whole of Western Europe as far as the Atlantic coast?

To put matters in their proper perspective, it should be emphasized that NATO has sufficient conventional forces in Europe to defend a front running from the Alps to the Baltic Sea and to back it up with appropriate operational reserves. Recent armament and training programmes comparable to the Soviet Union's modernization measures have enabled NATO to safeguard its defence options.

Both sides have been modernizing their equipment — a necessity imposed by continuous technological advances. The higher level of science and technology in the West has, however, increased NATO's qualitative advantage even further. NATO has clearly stepped up armaments recently, with the introduction of new ships and combat aircraft (among which is the distinctly offensive strike weapon, the MRCA Tornado), modern tanks, armoured infantry vehicles and reconnaissance tanks, new cannon and rocket artillery, new anti-aircraft and anti-tank weapons, new anti-tank helicopters, a new generation of wheeled vehicles and a new precision guidance system based on the most up-to-date communication engineering — to mention only the most important innovations.

There is no doubt that the Soviet Union has also introduced new weapons systems on a large scale in the last decade. They have improved their nuclear intermediate range weapons in particular, but also their land, air and maritime forces and, to a lesser degree, those of their allies, too. The Soviet Union, however, has failed to overtake the West in any significant field. In several important areas of war fighting capability, they have not even been able to catch up.

President Reagan's decision to step up armament was not necessary to secure the West's superiority in terms of quality or, so far as it is essential to NATO's aims, in terms of quantity. In view of this, General Christian Krause comes to the following conclusion:

If the Warsaw Pact want to attack NATO in Europe, it will first of all have to assemble superior armed forces. But it should not be forgotten that numerical superiority alone does not automatically guarantee the success of an attack. A well functioning defence front may be able to resist an aggressor who is numerically superior. The Warsaw Pact could only concentrate sufficient forces for an attack in Central Europe if the armoured divisions of its Satellites were mobilized, and further divisions sent from Western Russia. Without such measures, its military potential is not sufficient to attack NATO. . . . According to views prevailing in NATO Headquarters, the Warsaw Pact has a 'blitzkrieg doctrine', which means that the time for mobilizing and deploying troops is very short. In other words, its 33 armoured divisions would have to start their move to the front in a pre-mobilization state. According to 'Military Balance 1982/83', their state of readiness, however, is low. Only a quarter of the divisions deployed in European Russia are at more than 50 per cent strength needed for warfare, though we do not know the extent to which this shortfall applies to the 33 armoured divisions.

Lucas Fischer deals with this question in more detail in an Adelphi Paper published in the London Institute of Strategic Studies. He assumes that only 10 of the 33 divisions have more than 50 per cent of warfare capability. The remaining twenty are mere cadre units, and some of them are not fully equipped.

It is estimated that the time needed to mobilize Soviet reserve forces stationed in European Russia is about three weeks but these would not be first-class troops because reservists would have to be trained and would take time to reach the standard required. In addition, the headquarters staff required for the 33 divisions does not exist in peacetime and would have to be formed in the course of mobilization. It is not known what means of transport exist to transfer 33 divisions with 8,500 combat tanks across Poland and Czechoslovakia to the front line. When considering this question, it must be remembered that troop movements on this scale require the utmost precision if they are to be accomplished quickly. The slightest disruption could have disastrous consequences, which means that counter action by the enemy must be avoided at all costs. A Russian blitzkrieg doctrine, therefore, involves extremely rapid mobilization and deployment.

To air transport 8,500 tanks would be too costly and would take too long because of the planes' limited loading capacity. Transportation by land, on the other had, would only be possible for wheeled vehicles since the roads in those regions are generally not built to take the weight of tanks (a Russian combat tank weights approximately fifty tons). Sea routes could be used only by those divisions located near the coast. Consequently, the majority of troops would have to be transported by rail. However, the railway system in the Soviet Union and in the Eastern part of Central Europe has a low carrying capacity and an inadequate network of lines for normal traffic in peacetime, let alone in war. Since Russian railways are of a broader gauge than all other European railway networks, troop transports would have to be re-loaded at the Russian–Polish border, necessitating twice as many railway engines and special waggons for tank transportation. Finally, the whole enterprise would depend upon the reliability of the Polish and Czech railway administrations.

NATO could certainly break these transport lines at strategic points, particularly at the railway bridges over the rivers Vistula and Oder. The Vistula has at most four railway bridges suitable for military transports and the Oder only two. For several years NATO has been keeping missiles and aircraft in readiness to destroy these targets. Its ability to do so has been enhanced by the introduction of modern and extremely precise guided missiles. Thus, it is highly unlikely that the Soviet Union could transfer its divisions quickly and at full strength to a Central European combat zone.

Neither the state of readiness nor the transportability of the 33 divisions is sufficient for them to count as a major factor in the operational planning for an attack on Central Europe. These divisions are at best seen as a bonus for the Warsaw Pact and they certainly cannot be relied upon. It remains open to question whether, in the numbers game, they can be compared with the forces that NATO has stationed in Central Europe.

Measured against the requirements of a large-scale and rapid deployment, the extension of the railway network in Eastern bloc countries is progressing only slowly and spasmodically. The extent of the investment necessary to build up the railway network for military purposes is beyond the capacity of Eastern European countries. As an economic investment, it would also be counter-productive because the inter-economic relations within COMECON do not require such a sophisticated network.[22]

The 'numbers game' is used to manipulate facts and figures so as to give an impression of the superiority of Soviet forces in both quantity and quality. Comparisons are based on fire power, mobility and chances of survival. According to US estimates, the Warsaw Pact has an advantage over NATO in Central Europe of 1.2:1, i.e. a 20 per cent superiority in combat forces. A superiority of this size far from guarantees a successful attack factor since the attacker cannot concentrate his strike force in sufficient strength without weakening other sectors of his front.

Over the past fifteen years, the strength of the Warsaw Pact's forces have remained relatively constant, there even being a tendency to decrease it. In his annual report of 1982, US Secretary of Defense Weinberger pointed out that the numerical balance of forces and the quality of equipments do not represent any advantage in favour of the Warsaw Pact in Central Europe. Retired Admiral Gene La Rocque, Director of the Washington Center for Defense Information, has commented on the causes of exaggerated and unjustified speculation about the inferiority of NATO's armed forces. He was convinced, he said, that the constant uncertainty about American strength, fostered by Reagan and his advisers for years, was unsubstantiated and would damage America's position in the world. It must be understood that the USA was *not* weak, militarily, and that she and her allies were equal, if not superior, to the Warsaw Pact nations in all crucial aspects of military strength. The American President's obsession with nuclear armaments was a logical extention of his *idée fixe* that it was the Soviet Union who was responsible for the world's problems.[23]

One can but hope that Moscow is sufficiently informed to make a rather more realistic assessment of NATO's combat capability. Otherwise, NATO's 'weakness' would encourage the USSR to think that a Soviet armoured attack would present little risk of failing. However, the fundamental question remains as to whether a country's military potential can be orientated towards defence requirements or to the enemy's military potential. At first glance this question would seem of little importance but second thoughts show it to be of vital significance. National military preparations in terms of armament, armed forces deployment and training will meet the defence needs only if the principle of sufficiency is geared to the state's military objectives. The main task is to inflict such losses on an aggressor that they outweigh the expected gain. While recognizing that it is necessary to take account of the enemy's potential, if it were to be used as the sole criterion for planning one's own defence needs, it could create such anomalies as:

— a tendency towards 'over-armament', going beyond real defence needs;
— the tying of a country's military and armaments policy to that of the enemy;
— a comparison of armaments systems without taking compensating factors into account. For instance, comparing capabilities tank by tank or aircraft by aircraft, but neglecting to assess anti-tank or anti-aircraft components which may be cheaper to install than direct equivalents but
— which could lead to an obsession that an intolerable disparity exists in some areas;
— an inevitable increase in fears of threats on both sides and a reduction of the leeway for negotiating arms limitation and reduction, leading to a mutual stepping-up of the arms race.

Maxwell D. Taylor, Chairman of the Joint Chiefs of Staff in the early 1960s, a man who calls himself an 'unyielding hawk', criticizes precisely this aspect of the Reagan Administration's strategic policies. In a *Washington Post* article he suggested that the measure of sufficiency should not be the number of Soviet weapons but their destructive potential, measured in terms of America's security needs. At the same time, he contended that it would not further the development of strategic thinking to strive for parity of strategic weapons in every category (land-, sea- and air-based). According to Taylor, this sort of flawed logic led to the endorsement of the highly vulnerable MX missiles.[24]

Of these two security philosophies, the West has chosen to implement the decidedly more dangerous, more expensive and less productive policy. Our perception of the threat represented by the Soviet Union is not a realistic one and distracts us from resolving the problems which jeopardize our own survival and security. It would be better were we to take seriously the proposals put forward by the USSR and commit it to agreements and treaties, thus making its actions calculable.

There are enough examples, not only from the Second World War but also from the postwar era, to prove that the Soviet Union does keep agreements. The Austrian Treaty of 1955 is one situation in which the Soviet Union withdrew its forces and relinquished a sphere of influence. The Cuban crisis of 1962 is another example. McGeorge Bundy, security adviser to Presidents Kennedy and Johnson, recently wrote:

The most dangerous moment that America has had with the Russians, the Cuban missile crisis, was caused by terrible failures of perception on both sides and its peaceful resolution was the consequence not only of determination and strength but of intensive communication. Arms control negotiations have a much more complex history but the common testimony of American negotiators of all persuasions is that when Americans are serious, the Russians can be too. In less apocalyptic matters, we can find similar lessons. We know from nearly thirty years of Austrian freedom that these men can keep their word when they find it in their interest. The most sinister assumptions about chemical warfare and plots to kill cannot change these realities.[25]

The West has no reason and absolutely no right to put the Soviet Union in the dock alone. The list of our own mistakes is long and there is no reason to assume that it will not grow even longer. Algeria, Vietnam, the Lebanon, South Africa, Chile and El Salvador are only some of the regions and countries where economic and political interests tempted us to risk military engagements, instead of solving problems peacefully. Zambia's President Kenneth Kaunda pointed out quite rightly that military threats are not a suitable method of safeguarding 'natural resources'. Whatever political regime may be in power in the developing countries, they will always rely on trade with the West to solve their problems. The former head of the American delegation to the United Nations, Andrew Young, held similar views. He pointed out that a politically stable pro-Communist system offers better opportunities for political and economic co-operation than a pro-Western dictatorship whose survival can only be sustained by military and financial aid. Like many other US diplomats, Young was fired, probably because of his support for this sort of position. Instead the West relies on confrontation and wastes opportunities to solve our problems by peaceful means. Each year, 650 thousand million US dollars are spent for military purposes all over the world. A fraction of this huge sum would enable many of the problems that still claim millions of human lives to be solved — epidemic diseases, hunger and violence. Armament costs human lives, even without a war. It is time to end the destruction of human values and lives. It is time to pursue policies which, at least in Europe, do not lead from a postwar to a prewar period but to a stable peace.

The images we have created of our enemies prevent rational

political behaviour. Originally created to justify a policy of confrontation, they are beginning increasingly to determine our behaviour and make us prisoners of our own perceptions of threat, thus restricting our freedom of decision and action. By choosing military confrontation, we forego the opportunities provided by a proper use of political, economic and cultural relations. Much worse, however, is the fact that military confrontation is considered to be a major factor in international relations, leading very possibly to the destruction of us all.

From 'covert operations' to open conflict

The Reagan Administration's confrontation strategy has introduced another dangerous element into international relations, namely the direct, though sometimes covert, interference in the domestic affairs of other countries. During the 1982 State Department Conference already referred to, Secretary of State Shultz and his deputy Lawrence Eagleburger, announced that the US would increase her efforts to introduce a 'new era of democratic reform and revolution'. It was by no means an accident that the Conference was attended not only by diplomats and specialists but also by a large number of intelligence experts. This is reminiscent of earlier attempts to influence foreign states by covert activities which often led to international crises and conflicts. When the US Government had to set up a government commission in 1975 to investigate certain unconstitutional activities of the CIA, it became widely known that the United States had carried out more than 900 significant covert operations in foreign countries between 1961 and 1976. They included the Bay of Pigs invasion that failed in 1961, the officers' coup in the Dominican Republic in 1965, with the subsequent landing of US troops, and the support given to Pinochet when he overthrew the Chilean President Allende in 1973. In hundreds of cases on all continents, the United States played this risky game which can so quickly turn from covert operations into bloody war. On 8 November 1982, *Newsweek* claimed that a country with international responsibilities needs covert operations as a third strand of foreign policy, something stronger than diplomacy but less horrific than war. However, we must question whether covert activities really are less horrific than war. As long as they do not lead directly to open military confrontation, they differ from war only in scope. In terms of brutality, suffering and consequences for the people involved, they are nothing short of criminal. Sections of the armed forces are employed for these purposes, giving such operations a semi-warlike character. The Pentagon's defence directives for 1984–8 include reorganizing and strengthening forces for use in situations where the employment of US conventional forces would be either premature, inappropriate or impractical. 'Special forces', wrote the *New York Times* on 30 May 1982, 'is a euphemism for guerrillas, saboteurs, commando and other unconventional forces.' Since the 1950s, the term 'unconventional warfare' has been used in the USA's strategic planning for covert operations by military forces. It was an integral part of the Cold War and is again an essential element of a foreign policy based on confrontation.

Unconventional warfare has origins going back to the American War of Independence. After the Korean War, and particularly in the 1960s, the allied forces' experience of commando and guerrilla troops was thoroughly evaluated by NATO and developed as a military doctrine.

In his book *Guerrilla — Krieg ohne Fronten*, Professor Werner Halweg describes how the Supreme Command of the USA came to the conclusion that 'small wars' or 'guerrilla wars' could be an effective means of countering revolutions and uprisings in the under-developed countries wherever American interests were involved.[26] This became more important for the USA when the USSR caught up in nuclear weapons. The military leaders of the United States hoped to achieve their objectives by guerrilla warfare without having to risk a conventional or nuclear war.[27] In the USA, unconventional warfare, the military counterpart of secret service operations, includes the inter-related methods of guerrilla warfare, commando operations against a hostile country and the establishment of groups of resistance fighters. These operations are conducted on the territory of other countries in order to stimulate 'resistance movements' or uprisings against established governments and their armed forces. A US Army textbook contains the following passage:

A Resistance Movement is an organized effort by some portion of the civil population of a country to resist the legally established government or an occupying power. Initially such resistance may consist of subversive political activities and other actions designed to agitate and propagandize the populace to distrust and lose confidence in the legally established government or occupying power. If not suppressed, such resistance can result in insurgency by irregular forces.[28]

All NATO's armed forces today recognize the basic principle that conventional warfare, prepared from outside and carried through according to an agreed plan, aims to unsettle and, covertly, to overthrow legally established governments.

US President John F. Kennedy was one of the first American statesmen to realize the senseless and suicidal nature of a nuclear confrontation with the Warsaw Pact. Consequently, he preferred subtle tactical moves in negotiations with the Warsaw Pact to blunt confrontation. On the other hand, he and other politicians with similar ideas believed that unconventional warfare could become a decisive weapon against Communism. This explains why he subscribed to the view that the United States should be ready to seize any opportunity for taking the initiative in Poland or in other countries behind the Iron Curtain.[29] Advocates of covert operations and unconventional warfare against Communist countries today overlook the point of Kennedy's policy: that all of these means lose their justification if they increase the danger of nuclear confrontation. The defence directives of the Pentagon, however, reveal that the men around Caspar Weinberger consider unconventional warfare a preliminary stage of a hot war. The retired British General Sir John Hackett presents such a situation in a macabre way in his war scenario *The Third World War*. It narrates how NATO intelligence services organize unrest and armed uprisings in Warsaw Pact states as a preparation for military confrontation. One might say that literary imagination has carried Hackett beyond military reality but it is an entirely different matter when one reads, in a briefing paper for US armed forces in Europe, that operations of this kind are envisaged:

Bearing the initial brunt of this ambitious project in the European theatre would be several hundred expertly trained American soldiers now stationed in the quiet Bavarian town of Bad Tölz. As members of the 10th Special Forces Group (Airborne), these volunteers are ready and waiting for a signal that will send them anywhere from 200 to 2,000 miles inside enemy territory. Working in small detachments, they will there contact local groups of friendly guerrillas to begin military operations for which they have been thoroughly and uniquely trained.[30]

[52]

In the autumn of 1981, Norwegian newspapers released reports (based on US documents) that there are plans for commando troops to use chemical weapons and mini-nukes in the hinterland of the Warsaw Pact states. If this is the case, subversion, coups and uprisings could set off a war in Central Europe, with all the possibilities of escalation this involves. This calls into question the threat posed by the USA's methods of unconventional warfare since they challenge the democratic freedom of the European NATO countries. During the 1970s, the CIA and the US armed forces stepped up their efforts to establish bases for covert actions in allied European countries. Undercover agents were sent to Italy, France and Spain where domestic policies seemed to be in a state of flux. According to one of these agents, their main tasks were to prevent the Left from winning electoral victories and to recruit citizens of developing countries who were either residents or visitors to the country. In the establishment of covert operation bases, the US forces and military intelligence services like to use allied officers who have been trained in the rules of guerrilla warfare at US training camps. All Western armies contain thousands of officers and non-commissioned officers with this sort of training.

Apart from this, the USA is trying to reach legal agreements with its allies over unconventional warfare activities by secret service units and by the armed forces of their allies against a third party, for example, SACEUR agreements between the European Supreme Commander and Italy and West Germany. When they were signed on 9 February 1977, the *Süddeutsche Zeitung* wrote that, as early as the mid-1960s, USACEUR and the West German Government had planned a similar agreement. The plan, USCINCEUR OPLAN 100-1, had to be dropped because its contents were published by several newspapers and the whole matter had met with strong public resistance. Commanders of the US armed forces had hoped to secure guarantees which would give them a free hand for covert operations against Warsaw Pact states as well as against 'unstable' allied governments. But not one of the United States' partners was willing to give up as much sovereignty as the American plan demanded. In a state of emergency, every government wants to have the right to act independently. The majority of the allies certainly do not want to be drawn into political or military conflicts by covert operations. The SACEUR agreements are meant to provide the legal basis for this sort of activity in NATO countries. Keen observers of American political life were alarmed at one of President Reagan's first decisions after his inauguration on 20 January 1981. His proposal in Congress to abolish the Clark Amendment left all the advocates of unconventional warfare and covert operations jubilant. It meant the end of the temporary limitation of the intelligence services' covert operations — a measure which President Carter had felt to be necessary because of the Watergate affair and several unsuccessful CIA operations in foreign countries. While armaments were increased, unconventional warfare and the intelligence services received considerable encouragement.

There is general agreement among people close to the White House that under President Reagan the US intelligence services have received their strongest-ever peacetime support. The CIA was way out in front with a budget increase of 25 per cent in the 1983 financial year. President Reagan's Order No. 12333 gave the intelligence services more leeway. The CIA's department for special operations and its mobile forces — Special Operations Division (SOD) — were strengthened. In the *New York Times Magazine* of 16 January 1983, Philip Taubman reported on the CIA's largest paramilitary and political operation in the last ten years. The CIA claims that its operations in Nicaragua are strictly under control and are limited to harassing the Sandinistas. According to Taubman, however, there is ample proof that the CIA is involved in a secret war against the Leftist Sandinistas. The CIA provides money, training facilities and military equipment for paramilitary units, mostly controlled by exile groups. Taubman points out that this programme is particularly alarming because it is incompatible with the declared US policy of settling regional problems with Nicaragua at the negotiating table and goes beyond the secret operation plans recently sanctioned by President Reagan.

At present, the CIA is involved in similar activities in many countries, including Guatemala, El Salvador, Honduras, Zaire, Sudan, Afghanistan, Angola, Nicaragua and Poland. Another indication of intensification in the underground war is the formation of a Central Command for Special Warfare, initiated by the President in the autumn of 1982. Its task is to co-ordinate all the unconventional units of the Army, Navy, Air Force and the Marines. These include:
— the Special Forces of the Army, which have been increased from 3,600 to 5,000 men. The Army's Ranger battalions have also been assigned to them. The Special Forces' main tasks include the training of officers for special units in other countries, the training of rebels and guerrilla fighters for tasks in the territories of hostile

countries and the engagement of American soldiers behind enemy lines;

— the Special Operations Wing of the Air Force. These units support and supply guerrilla troops from the air and, according to their commander, Colonel Lox, they are very busy at present and 'will be even busier' in the future.
— the Special Units of the Navy (SEALS). From the sea they carry out acts of sabotage and support underground fighters. They include about 400 'reconnaissance' marines who have largely been withdrawn from their original duties and are being prepared and used for covert operations.

In its Document MC 14/3, issued in the early 1960s, NATO declared that covert operations were a part of its plans and objectives. Following this, several allied countries established similar units or increased the number of existing ones. France has several regiments of commando infantry as well as special action forces within its intelligence service, DGSE. Great Britain has its Special Air Service, Special Boat Service and its intelligence services' Special Political Actions (SPA) groups for secret operations and unconventional warfare. There are particularly strong connections between unconventional warfare forces and mercenaries operating openly against developing Third World countries. In covert operations, specialists from the US Special Forces prepare the recruitment, financing, training and infiltration of mercenaries into Angola, Mozambique and Zaire (previously the Congo). The advantage of this type of connection between unconventional units and mercenaries is that if a mercenary operation miscarries, the great powers can deny any involvement and avoid international complications.

Commando units and similar special forces engaged in unconventional warfare are nothing new but in past wars their raids behind enemy lines were a part of military operations and complied with the laws of war. At present, unconventional warfare is being used for dubious missions that endanger peaceful international cooperation. According to the American conception, the objectives of unconventional forces in peacetime are to prevent 'successive escalation of the influence of the Soviets and their satellites' and to 'support friendly nations when American interests are at stake in their countries'.[31]

In recent years we have had ample opportunity to see how far from reality are the suspicions held by the American Administration and also by the governments of other countries that the 'evil hand of

[55]

Moscow' is at work behind every assertive move in Third World states. It is a mistake either to ignore or deny the social causes of political unrest in Latin American countries but it is the USA's habit to blame the USSR for them, applying a kind of political blackmail as a means of establishing bilateral international relations. The dangers inherent in this strategy are illustrated in an admission by Zbigniew Brzezinski, Security Adviser to President Carter. Brzezinski revealed that there had been plans to provide an incident with a Soviet ship in order to disguise the failure of an American commando assignment against Iran in 1980. Who knows where this sort of covert operation may lead?

As long as the West uses unconventional forces, new causes of international conflicts and stalemate in negotiations with the Soviet Union will be created. Meanwhile, the nuclear arms race is escalating and that is reason enough to drop this dangerous game with unconventional warfare which only poisons the international atmosphere and obstructs negotiations. Let us not forget that the Helsinki Final Act requires all signatory states 'to refrain from acts of military occupation or other direct or indirect measures of violence against the territory of a member state'.[32] We have tried to show what might be in store for Europe if we follow unconditionally the Reagan Administration's policies. We have not forgotten our experience of the Cold War in the 1950s. At that time the United States was already behaving as if it had a divine mission to destroy the Communist system. The USSR motivation to become a super-power emerged from that period in the 1950s when there was an almost total absence of political communication, an unwillingness to negotiate, a vacuum in trade relations and, not least, a strong anti-Communist lobby in the West. It was during that time that the USSR created its vast industrial potential and the scientific resources which enabled it to break the American nuclear monopoly and to launch the first sputnik into space.

The states of the Eastern bloc rallied around the Soviet Union and the Warsaw Pact seemed transformed into a monolithic bloc. In the phase of its formation, when difficult conditions had to be overcome and opposing political forces had to be disciplined, the West contributed directly to the consolidation of the Pact's structure. The West first wanted to contain and then to roll back Communism. It did not succeed and finally had to accept the limits of its capabilities. The Cold War of the 1950s cost the West dear. It led to economic losses, to an arms race which makes no sense, economically or socially, and to the military–industrial complex. It led to discrimination and deterioration in intellectual standards and at times threatened individual rights of freedom of thought and action. Today, the situation is no better but the risks are higher. By believing that we can change the Communist system from outside and by force endangers not only ourselves but the whole world. In the end it will have to be recognized that our survival will depend on our ability to reach agreements.

There is but one way to decrease the tensions that have brought us to the brink of a Hot War — a return to the policy of détente and balance. As former President Nixon said, it was not détente itself that had failed but its implementation by American politicians.

A policy of détente is not a concession to the Soviet Union, but a matter of survival for the states of Western Europe as well as for the United States of America. People in Washington cannot assume that they are far enough away to survive the result of a policy of confrontation — a nuclear inferno. Those times have gone for ever.

We should also remember that, while the Reagan Administration's policy of confrontation threatens the Soviet Union, it also threatens the existence of NATO. NATO was created to defend the fundamental security interests of its member states, not to expose them to dangers resulting from a crusade mentality. In the past, as much as today, security meant respecting the basis of the North Atlantic Treaty.

Is Suicide a Defence?

NATO's nuclear plans

King Pyrrhus' experience in battle has taught us that there is no victory where the losses outweigh the gains. If the results for Europe of the First and Second World Wars are considered from this point of view, the value of war as a means of achieving political objectives appears highly dubious. At the end of the Second World War, American political scientists rightly pointed out that under present conditions war is no longer a continuation of policies by other means but represents the end of politics altogether. In view of the deployment of mass armies, the increased destruction potential of weapons and their industrial production, war — which previously had been regarded as a legitimate instrument of politics — had to be re-defined. With the development of nuclear arms capable of mass destruction, the problem arose of how to control this newly-created potential, instead of being controlled by it. The human race, divided into attackers and defenders, now finds itself in the same situation as Goethe's sorcerer's apprentice. Both sides are equally threatened by the new weapons of mass destruction. This became obvious after the explosions of the atom bombs on Hiroshima and Nagasaki but it has hardly influenced the political and military thinking since.

No account has been taken of the fact that since the US monopoly on atomic weapons was broken, so that now both super-powers possess them, no rational use can be made of these weapons for attack or defence. Their new qualitative powers of destruction make them as unsuited for securing a defence policy as a car spanner is for repairing a wrist-watch. It is time to give up the idea of basing security policy on military concepts and turn instead to political means. Arsenals of nuclear weapons should have been limited immediately and strategies developed in accordance with the new reality of a destructive power hitherto unknown. What happened was that thinking continued along the same old lines and military potential and strategic factors were still used as political instruments.

America's first nuclear weapons had been designed for use in warfare and were employed thus at Hiroshima and Nagasaki but, when the United States lost her nuclear monopoly, the function of these weapons necessarily had to be re-evaluated. The 'strategy of massive retaliation' which involved the early use of nuclear weapons in any serious conflict was short-lived. Nuclear weapons had been regarded as super-bombs that would guarantee victory over any adversary, in particular the Soviet Union. However, as the Soviet Union developed nuclear weapons and delivery systems which made the USA itself vulnerable to attack, the USA's options of using nuclear arms as a means of warfare decreased.

The strategy of massive retaliation was a strategy of nuclear warfare and represented the principle of unilateral deterrence. The step from unilateral to mutual deterrence turned nuclear armament into a limited preventive measure. The development of mutual deterrence meant that any use of nuclear weapons involved — initially — a calculated prohibitive risk. Eventually, the enemy's capability to retaliate meant that the use of nuclear weapons brought with it the threat of self-annihilation. The threat of assured mutual destruction raised questions of how to stabilize the situation in the interests of survival. Nuclear weapons were regarded more cautiously, only to be used as a last resort. This system, based on mutual fear, was far from providing a stable and peaceful order.

In the early 1960s, the Cuban crisis had emphasized the necessity of a moderate and cautious handling of strategic nuclear decisions. It became obvious that the USA's strategic nuclear superiority could not be used to solve conflicts solely in the interests of the stronger side. Even from its position of relative inferiority at that time, the Soviet Union could still threaten the United States with damage at an unacceptable level in the event of war. That signified the end of the strategy of massive retaliation because it no longer met the USA's — and therefore NATO's — strategic requirements.

The development of the strategy of flexible response reflects this process of change, in which the emphasis was put more on potential response than on the active use of nuclear weapons. The nuclear capabilities of both super-powers increasingly neutralized each other thus requiring compromise and mutual restraint.

While the earlier strategy had involved the use of nuclear weapons in every conflict, the new one was based on the idea that a war could be waged with conventional weapons either until a victory was won, thus making nuclear weapons superfluous, or a defeat had to be averted by resorting to nuclear weapons. The slogan was: employ nuclear weapons as late as possible and as early as necessary. This meant, however, that the development of nuclear arms for use in warfare received a strong boost and became an integral part of strategic thinking. The division between strategic and tactical nuclear operations had far-reaching consequences; the dilemma of NATO's nuclear strategy originated in this kind of approach. Firstly, it diverted attention from the fact that a nuclear war would result in unacceptable losses for both sides. The idea that a limited nuclear war could be fought and won without initiating an overall nuclear conflagration became regarded as feasible. Secondly, nuclear superiority could have political advantages. By defeating the enemy on the battlefield, with or without nuclear weapons, war could once again fulfil its classic function as an instrument of politics. Thirdly, strategic perceptions about the practicalities of using nuclear weapons were confirmed when deterrence — the ability to inflict unacceptable damage on the enemy — was found to be no longer essential. The conviction grew that nuclear weapons could be employed against military targets only; meaning that the military function of waging and winning a nuclear war was once again plausible.

As this re-orientation towards maximum deterrence took place, strategic concepts involving the threat of a preventive disarming strike developed. Consequently, the production of nuclear weapons was increased. They were no longer considered political weapons of mutual deterrence but once again were seen as a means of waging war. Their numbers were no longer calculated according to the extent of damage considered unacceptable for the enemy but according to the number of military targets. In this context there has been a transition from a 'counter-value-strategy', aimed at towns and industrial centres, to a 'counter-force-strategy', aimed at the enemy's military potential. In reality, however, neither of these strategies has ever existed in exact terms. Target lists have always included civilian as well as military targets and the use of nuclear weapons against them has always been part of the plan. The change in strategies can be considered more a quantitative shift from one target group to another. It would be totally wrong to deduce any decrease in the extent of danger to the civilian population.

The history of NATO reveals that its strategy eventually has always followed that of the USA. It is therefore not surprising that the concept central to the USA's nuclear war strategy is reflected in that of NATO. This, however, raises another question. The United States is a super-power with a huge nuclear capability but the other NATO countries are not. The deployment of US nuclear weapons in Europe does not threaten the existence of the USA — if it is limited to this region — but it does represent a threat to the existence of the European NATO states who would have to bear the brunt of any attack. The United States pursues a global policy with all the military consequences that this involves whereas the countries of Western Europe pursue largely regional objectives. NATO's internal state and the debates about strategy are therefore not merely the result of different political and military views but also the result of fundamentally different political and military conditions, interests and opportunities in the various NATO countries.

The point has been reached where the armed forces of the West and East are being classified under three headings: conventional, theatre nuclear and strategic nuclear. The United States' intention is to deploy its strategic nuclear weapons in approximately equal propor-tions — in the air (bombers), at sea (submarines) and on land (silos). The Soviet Union, however, did not follow the same proportional subdivisions but placed their confidence in the land-based systems as having the best survival and penetration capabilities.

In the autumn of 1977, Paul Nitze published a revealing survey of the steps by which a potential conflict could escalate.[1] His analysis was in terms of the 'war profiles' of the flexible response strategy. Later, in 1982, public opinion reacted strongly, both to Secretary of State Haig's suggestion that a 'token single nuclear strike' could act as a demonstration of the USA's intent to use nuclear weapons if necessary, and to President Reagan's comments on the winning of a limited nuclear war. It is of interest to note that Nitze, who had voiced the same ideas five years earlier, was by then President Reagan's chief arms control negotiator. This is the survey Nitze published:

Level	Sub-level	Type of war—level of deterrence	Weapons used
O	1	In space (limited, but of strategic nature)	Nuclear or conventional (laser, FOBS, satellites and anti-satellite missiles)
A	2	Nuclear intercontinental, counter-value	ICBM, SLBM, strategic bombers
	3	Nuclear intercontinental, counter-force	Cruise missiles
B	4	Nuclear theatre (regional), counter-value	Eurostrategic weapons: IRBM/MRBM, medium-range bombers (Backfire, FB 111)
	5	Nuclear theatre (regional), counter-force	FBS, intermediate-range Cruise missiles
C	6	Nuclear, confined to advanced zones of contact with the enemy	Only short-range tactical nuclear weapons with low throw weight (ADM, neutron bomb, etc. exclusively counter-force)
	7	Nuclear, confined to unilateral use of tactical nuclear weapons in self-defence on national territory	
	8	Conventional, with both super-powers directly involved at the same time	Conventional weapons
	9	Conventional, with only one super-power directly involved	
	10	Conventional, with allies or client states involved	
E	11	Civil and guerrilla war in various forms	Chiefly light weapons
F	12	Economic, political and psychological warfare	

Scenarios like this create the dangerous illusion that a conflict will escalate only as far as we want it to and that the enemy will react in response to our signals and behave in a rational way. In the case of a conflict, this line of reasoning expects the Soviet Union to display a degree of rationality which it is denied they possess. Is not the Soviet Union's rejection of this agreement more honest than our concept of deterrence which merely simulates a rational attitude? This faulty premise leads to further misconception. The resulting analysis is not based on reality but on assumptions about the enemy's possible reactions, on anxieties and on articles of faith.

A new and rational security policy urgently needs to be developed which takes account of the quantitative and qualitative weapon factors and their threat to mankind's very existence. It is, however, not so much that the security policy has to be changed to take account of the altered conditions but rather the ways and means by which the objectives are to be achieved. These objectives are:

— to guarantee national existence;
— to safeguard the territorial integrity and the inviolability of a country's borders;
— to guarantee freedom of political decision-making and state sovereignty in all essential areas.

National security interests determine the existence of a military alliance like NATO. Its stability and continued existence are possible only if all, or at least most, of the member states recognize its usefulness for the maintenance of their own national security interests. Grave doubts about its benefits, or attempts by one state to secure its own specific security interests at the expense of the other member states, must ultimately lead to confusion and crises.

American military policy and, above all, American nuclear strategic thinking, clearly tends towards a unilateralism which is centred exclusively on American interests. Some US politicians hold the view that America should not have to take account at all of NATO's interests but that NATO should recognize the USA's global responsibilities and comply with its policies and demands. US Secretary of Defense Weinberger and UN Ambassador Jeane Kirkpatrick are among those politicians who are motivated by this new American self-confidence and awareness of a mission. UN Ambassador Kirkpatrick pointed out recently that the ambitions of NATO are irrelevant to some central aspects of US foreign policy.[2] The few people in the United States who plead for more consideration of European interests are obviously in the minority but, even among them, only the odd one would publicly state that current military planning and war scenarios cannot ensure the security of Europe or the United States and that it is time there was a return to political methods of conflict resolution and containment.

In the United States, as well as in other member states of NATO,

[63]

doubts are growing about the fundamental ideas on which the Pentagon's strategic planning and Washington's foreign policy are based. This increasingly open dissent has produced what is cautiously described as a 'sharpening of the debate on NATO's strategy'. In fact, it is no longer merely a debate on strategies but the expression of definite reservations about a foreign and defence policy that is neither rational nor realistic. It is dividing NATO to an extent which, if unchecked, could lead to a crisis in the Alliance.

The main issues of the controversy arise from doubts about Washington's claims:

— that the USSR is strategically superior in important military fields;
— that we must achieve military supremacy in order to negotiate with the Soviet Union about arms control and disarmament from a position of strength;
— that military superiority can be achieved and that the Soviet Union can thereby be forced into submission;
— that a nuclear war — if it cannot be limited to the European theatre of war — would last for several months and could be won by the United States.

In the autumn of 1981, President Carter's directive PD59 was amended by a Pentagon directive, extracts of which were published in the *New York Times* on 30 May 1982. It is not the only example of the 'nuclear victory is possible' attitude held by many military leaders and politicians. It is supplemented and expressed more precisely in the forces' manuals FM100-5 and 101-31, as well as in the two Air-Land-Battle doctrines covering air force and ground forces, the planning of air and ground forces cooperation and coordination, and air force planning into the twenty-first century. These directives give substance to Colin S. Gray's and Keith Payne's misleading slogan, 'victory is possible', and form the basis of a philosophy which equates with the views of Edward Teller, the father of the hydrogen bomb, who believes that a nuclear war is not as horrible as is commonly assumed. Teller claims that the radio-active fall-out will be endurable after about 100 days and therefore comprehensive civil defence measures would make such a war feasible. After all, as he recalls, trams were running again in Hiroshima after only three days.

In view of the cynicism which considers 20 million dead among the US population — not to mention the total destruction of Western Europe — an appropriate price for wiping Communism from the face of the earth, US strategy and its objectives do not provide a basis on which there can be a consensus. The aim of NATO's strategic and military planning cannot and must not be to substitute attack for defence — it is compatible with the Statutes of neither NATO nor the United Nations to threaten the political and military centres of other states with nuclear 'decapitating strikes' because we do not like their political systems. Nor is it an acceptable or realistic form of conflict resolution.

The continuing build-up of arsenals and the development of new 'strategies for nuclear victory' suggest that military and political thinking is far behind military technology. This is the only explanation for the fact that nuclear weapons figure prominently in plans for a military victory over Communism. Their function as instruments for mututal deterrence and for the prevention of war was undermined when the Americans gave up maintaining mutual destructive capabilities in favour of military and nuclear superiority. When the United States discarded the philosophies which had been fundamental to SALT II, new and dangerous nuclear arms systems and new attitudes towards their implementation were created as a matter of course.

Even under the favourable conditions provided by a mutual readiness to cooperate in maintaining an approximate strategic balance, SALT left a number of destabilizing elements, including:
— the extension of MIRV technology, that is the capability to hit several targets at one strike;
— increasing the number of nuclear warheads and improving their accuracy;
— the introduction of civil defence measures and the improvement of anti-missile defence systems;
— technological breakthroughs in other branches of strategic armament.

As nuclear weapons were no longer seen as instruments of mutual deterrence but were considered to be for active use in waging war, technological developments increased in significance. As a result the following tendencies in weapon development emerged:

1. Miniaturization of nuclear weapons
These are nuclear weapons of reduced size and effect. Nuclear grenade shells have already been developed for 155mm howitzers. Their explosive power is approximately one-tenth of that of the atom bomb dropped on Hiroshima. Research is being done on the size and effect of

these miniature nuclear weapons so that they can interact with conventional weapons. Obviously, this development raises problems of control within the context of arms limitation and disarmament measures. Nuclear weapons as small as this can easily be concealed and thus may evade verification. If they are used, it is possible that their effects may be confused with those produced by conventional weapons, as the range of effects in each case overlaps.

2. *Selective use of nuclear weapons*

The overall effect of nuclear weapons is a complex combination of explosive and heat effects, electro-magnetic radiation and particle radiation. One example of the selective use of this range is the development of weapons of enhanced radiation, i.e. the neutron bomb, whose explosive and heat effects have been reduced whereas the neutron-induced radiation effect of a nuclear explosion has been increased.

Another variation which increases the explosive effect is the weapon group known as 'earth-penetrators'. They were developed with the objective of destroying targets concealed in bunkers, i.e. enemy command posts and missile sites.

3. *Selective nuclear warheads*

Nuclear warheads can be fitted with a variety of devices which vary the strength of the explosion and which can be selected before launching. The development of all these categories is ample proof that they are intended for military use and not for political deterrence. Weapons with selective explosive yields simplify storage because it is no longer necessary to keep specific nuclear warheads in readiness for each task. The number and effectiveness of nuclear warheads can, by this means, be considerably increased.

The development of delivery systems is as important as that of warheads. Apart from increased mobility, micro-electronics has opened up completely new possibilities, which have been exploited recently by the United States. The improvement in accuracy achieved by means of various active and passive electronic devices, which can also be used for conventional systems, is of great significance. The development of the Cruise missiles and Pershing II illustrates the progress in this field. (However, the failure in tests of both Cruise and Pershing is around 30 per cent, unacceptably high for operational reliability and predictability.) They now have an average target deviation of 30 metres which, in the next generation of Cruise missiles, is to be reduced to 10 metres. Thus, it is possible to destroy point targets, that is, political or miltary command centres and missile sites. As important as their improved accuracy is the increased penetration capability of the electronically-controlled delivery systems. These weapons are designed:

— to fly underneath radar surveillance;
— to minimize the radar echo;
— to obstruct or prevent the detection and destruction of these delivery systems by means of electronic counter measures.

Considerable progress has been made in the field of target programming. A few years ago the input of target coordinates for the various kinds of delivery systems took several hours and it was extremely difficult to set coordinates for moving targets. This time has been reduced to minutes, allowing a fast and flexible response in nuclear target planning.

In the light of these new developments, statements by leading US politicians, which had originally been regarded as mere propaganda, have increasingly turned into definite nuclear strategic plans. The idea that it is possible to defeat the Soviet Union and wipe out its political system in a nuclear war — even if it cannot be localized — was developed in a whole series of documents beginning with Carter's Presidential Directive PD59. This was followed by the Pentagon's guideline document, the forces' manuals FM100-5 and 101-31 and, finally, the US Army's new doctrine of Air–Land–Battle.

Strategies for nuclear victory are embedded in a complex military plan. Its basic hypothesis is that the threat of massive nuclear retaliation — made possible by strategic parity — may not deter the Soviet Union from using its superiority in a few specific fields to launch a limited but massive conventional or nuclear attack. In view of the threat of mutual annihiliation, the USSR might stop but are unlikely to allow any change in the new status quo. For this reason, the United States must achieve at least parity, preferably superiority, in all military areas. These are the premises of the 'countervailing' strategy which determines NATO's current military and armaments policies. It has given rise to fears which have been expressed by retired US Admiral John Marshall Lee.

Lee suggests that a countervailing strategy might lower the nuclear threshold. If someone is forced to take action — any action — then the

[67]

mere existence of nuclear options might provide the impetus to push the human race over the fateful brink from conventional to nuclear war.

Lee's second concern is that limited nuclear actions could lend support to the illusion that a nuclear war can be controlled. Of course, no one can say for certain what will happen in a nuclear war. We know that it will be disastrous. However, we can predict that, should a total nuclear war begin, at whatever level, there will be no chance of preventing ultimate annihilation. All limited options depend upon faultless control of the operation, timed to within minutes, on a great deal of information being available and on a host of controllers, dispersed at a number of locations — all of them under extreme pressure — functioning with the utmost efficiency. In the meantime, parts of the system would have been destroyed by enemy attacks. Under these conditions, a controlled and precise implementation of military operations plans is unimaginable. Furthermore — and this is even less likely to happen — the two sides in a nuclear war would have to coordinate their actions if a limited operation were to work, that is, if both sides were successfully to stop their exchange of nuclear strikes before mutual annihilation. All this would have to happen while conventional or nuclear fighting was actually taking place. Both sides would have to recognize and accept approximately the same operational limits and strike only at targets of the same type and level. They would have to accept the same result — and all this while acting under frightening degrees of stress and pressure of time, guided by different information and different plans, using different weapons and pursuing diametrically opposed objectives. It is difficult to imagine that success could be possible under these circumstances.

Lee's third concern is that a countervailing strategy encourages an unlimited strategic arms race. Although strategic weapons have a limited strike-back capability, they are relatively inflexible as a means of war and some parts of the system can function only for a limited time. If, however, the capability for massive strikes is to be maintained, a wide spectrum of plans is required which in turn requires a wide variety of weapons and especially accurate strike-back weapons.

Lee's fourth concern is that, since its inception, NATO has relied on nuclear weapons to counter what it perceives as the USSR's conventional superiority. In fact, NATO expects more of nuclear arms than is feasible and it will continue to do so. Thirty years ago, when there were only a few nuclear weapons and most of them were in our possession, it may have been a convincing strategy. Since the arsenals on both sides have grown enormously, countervailing has become recognised as an imprudent, alarming and unrealistic strategy.[3]

General David C. Jones, former Chairman of the US Joint Chiefs of Staff, warned at the time of his retirement in June 1983 that any attempt to prepare for a long nuclear war against the Soviet Union would mean pouring money down the drain. At the same time, he voiced his doubts as to whether a nuclear conflict between USSR and the United States could be contained. He believed it would lead inevitably to an all-out exchange of nuclear strikes.[4] General Jones, however, pointed primarily to the financial aspect of the problem. The idea that security can be based on a policy of strength and superiority requires more consideration.

(a) The notion that military superiority is possible is unrealistic in view of the existing nuclear arsenals and delivery vehicles. The explosion of only a fraction of the existing strategic systems would result in extremely heavy damages for the states concerned.

(b) A security concept based on a policy of strength is possible only at the expense of other countries and would result in a curtailment of international security. It consciously takes into account a dimunition of the security of the West European allies, the Warsaw Pact countries and the non-aligned nations.

(c) A security concept which cold-bloodedly calculates the death of millions of people and risks the very existence of the human race is incompatible with our political and moral standards.

(d) Any policy of strength interferes with the legitimate interests of other states. It will be perceived as a threat and will inevitably result in counter-measures. Provoking an arms race will not only result in the failure of military and political objectives; it will also undermine any chance of finding political solutions to conflicts and thus will pave the way for extremely dangerous, preventive defence strategies.

Demonstrations of strength and the objective of achieving strategic nuclear superiority cannot provide the basis for a security policy. They can only produce insecurity. They will lead to a new stage in the arms race and will undermine the options of arms control and disarmament, thus putting the very foundation of our security at risk. In a speech to the Council of Foreign Relations, US Secretary of Defense Caspar Weinberger demanded that we should be prepared to counter any expression of the Soviet Union's military power. If deterrence is of no avail, we must be capable of winning a war in order to survive.[5]

[69]

Colin S. Gray publicly declared that an American victory is possible in a nuclear war: 'If American nuclear power is to support US foreign policy objectives, the United States must possess the ability to wage nuclear war rationally'.[6] Statements of this sort reveal the full extent of this frightening and irrational approach.

Admiral Lee was correct in assuming that very few Americans believe either that one side can win a nuclear war, or that nuclear war is a positive means of achieving national objectives. The few who appear still to believe this, however, include the President of the United States and his Secretary of Defence. It could be a decisive factor in an assessment of the situation — and not only from Moscow's point of view. The global strategy concepts outlined in the Pentagon's guideline documents have been supplemented by several other military directives, with particular attention to Europe. These clearly reveal the intentions of Reagan, Weinberger and Co. In the forces' manual FM100-1 we read:

> In those situations which affect significantly vital US interests, our political authorities may consider use of American military power. This means that the United States must prepare itself for the use of military power across the entire spectrum of conflict, from relatively mild policy disagreements to fairly intense non-warfare confrontations of an economic or political nature, leading to a range of military situations which could conceivably include nuclear war.[7]

When the Air–Land–Battle doctrine became official, to be reinforced by the armed forces' manuals FM 100-5 and 101-31, in 1982, the American weekly *US-News and World Report* reacted with restraint, remarking that Air–Land–Battle creates the impression that a US attack is feasible. In fact, this is the first US Army doctrine which comprehensively integrates conventional, chemical and nuclear warfare in an offensive strategy.

Air–Land–Battle-2000 is the futuristic variant of these earlier military doctrines, extending into the year 2000. It contains the plans for war and considerations which Pentagon strategists consider might be relevant at the beginning of the next century. To disregard these plans as pure nonsense is dangerous because they make detailed demands of the US armament industry which are intended to ensure that America retains the initiative in military matters.

All these military plans focus on the European theatre of war.

[70]

Colonel Werner, a spokesman for the Army Training and Doctrine Command (TRADOC), emphasized that this doctrine is to be put into effect on the border between East and West Germany so that an immediate offensive can be undertaken against the Warsaw Pact.[8] It is obvious that considerations like these do not reassure the European allies. On the contrary, Europeans are becoming increasingly convinced that Air–Land–Battle and FM100-1 are strategic concepts designed to implement US policy objectives by military means.

The centrepiece of the Air–Land–Battle doctrine is a strategy of deep strikes against the Warsaw Pact forces' second line of defence, far into the enemy's hinterland. FM100-5 contends that small units attacking quickly with nuclear or chemical weapons could achieve the same results as larger units armed with conventional weapons. The use of nuclear and chemical weapons in the initial phase of an attack could reduce the fighting power of the enemy to such an extent that deep-striking multiple and co-ordinated attacks become feasible.[9] The conventional component of this strategy, known in Western Europe as the Rogers Plan, has not been conceived as a conventional alternative to the use of nuclear weapons but in the hope of convincing a naïve and ill-informed public as to its credibility as an alternative. The Rogers Plan in fact is designed to supplement nuclear with conventional superiority. It is to be achieved by using computers, communications and reconnaissance systems as well as automatically targeting conventional weapon systems.

An article in *Military Review* pointed out, quite correctly, that FM100-5 provides not only for a first *use* of nuclear weapons but also for the possibility of a nuclear first *strike*. That there is a subtle difference between the terms 'first use' and 'first strike' will be of no consequence to the areas affected. 'First use' would follow conventional battles that were going badly for America and NATO; 'first strike', on the other hand, means a preventive surprise first use of nuclear weapons in a conflict situation which need not necessarily be purely military. A nuclear first strike might take place in a situation where there has not been any prior fighting.

One can only fear the worst when US military leaders request the American President to make an early issue of theatre nuclear weapons to military command headquarters. Daniel Ellsberg, former adviser to ex-US Defense Secretary Robert McNamara , let it be known that, in 1957, President Eisenhower, and later Presidents Kennedy and Johnson, had authorized some American commanders to decide independently about the use of nuclear weapons under certain circumstances. A journal published by the Swedish Peace and Arbitration Association in September 1982 listed eleven instances between 1946 and 1972 when the United States had overtly or covertly considered the use of nuclear weapons. In at least some of these instances, it may be assumed that the United States did not refrain from action because of moral considerations but because of the existing Soviet nuclear capability that did in fact have a deterrent effect in these cases.

Nuclear weapons are allotted a crucial role in a military victory over Communism. The decision to employ them, however, is a matter of military jurisdiction. Civilians such as ministers and parliamentarians have no insight into the process of military decision-making. This is partly due to NATO's structure, which is subdivided into a political and a military branch. Any one who has ever held a high-ranking military position in NATO knows that military planning is kept separate from political decisions and influences, thus preserving the autonomy of military decision-making. NATO's military echelons act relatively independently of political and situational assessments. Day-by-day plans are made, measures introduced and decisions taken — usually based on 'worst case' scenarios — that influence politics much more than they are influenced in return. The structural subdivision of NATO into two branches that function relatively independently of each other has led to a situation in which military plans increasingly overrule political objectives and may no longer be under political control. Governments and parliamentarians can at best influence the amount of military expenditure or see to it that the armaments lobby gets this or that contract. They are rarely in a position to judge the political implications of military plans and decisions because they do not have the appropriate technical knowledge. Any expert on NATO matters knows that this situation is being exploited by the United States. It is not surprising therefore that West European governments feel rather apprehensive about Washington taking any important action on its own initiative. Such concern stems directly from this contemporary American policy and is understandable since the Supreme Commander of NATO's European forces, General Rogers, has set about persuading the European allies as to the merits of American strategy. It represents a definite attempt to put Reagan's and Weinberger's anti-Soviet direct confrontation strategy into practice, not only politically and ideologically but also militarily.

Anyone who has grasped the implications of the use of nuclear weapons of mass destruction must recognize the grave dangers inherent in these policies. Whatever strategic concept these attitudes serve, their dangerous and irresponsible character remains.

In an article in *Foreign Affairs*, the historian Michael Howard pointed out the necessity for West European states to free themselves from political and military dependence on US nuclear weapons.

> What is needed today is a reversal of that process whereby European governments have sought greater security by demanding an ever greater intensification of the American nuclear commitment; demands that are as divisive within their own countries as they are irritating for the people of the United States. Instead, we should be doing all that we can to reduce our dependence on American nuclear weapons by enhancing, so far as is militarily, socially and economically possible, our capacity to defend ourselves.[10]

Professor Howard's comments serve to emphasize that from the very beginning, US nuclear weapons have been the decisive element in NATO's strategy development. At the same time they have been the means by which the USA has maintained and expressed its leading role in political and military affairs. This leading role is necessary and acceptable so long as it represents, and takes account of, the national security interests of all NATO members. However, the United States is putting its own position in doubt by pursuing a policy of shared risk in the Alliance, the greater part of which is to be borne by Western Europe and other regions. European politicians should realise what is being demanded of them by this new American strategy which is about to become general NATO policy.

Nuclear strategies and the super-powers' ambitions

It is important to establish that the significance of the American nuclear capability within NATO increased as the Soviet nuclear potential grew, neutralizing the superiority of US nuclear forces. The West European states considered American nuclear weapons as a counterweight to the conventional and nuclear military power of the USSR. Changes of nuclear strategy in the United States, and subsequently in NATO, were however less the result of co-ordination between the North Atlantic allies than of America's reactions to changes in the nuclear strategic balance *vis-à-vis* the USSR. In other words, decisive decisions for change in America's, and therefore NATO's, nuclear strategies were not the result of a clear definition and co-ordination of the Alliance's defence interests. They were dictated by the development of the Soviet Union's nuclear capability and the limitations this imposed on the employment of US nuclear arms.

Western Europeans could not ignore the statements of leading American politicians like Henry Kissinger, who has said openly that it is unrealistic to expect the United States to use strategic nuclear weapons in defence of the European allies and thus risk Soviet retaliation against American territory. Neither did 'nuclear co-operation' in NATO's Nuclear Planning Group (NPG) help to solve problems resulting from the unequal sharing of the nuclear risk within the Alliance. Whilst member states of the Western Alliance may have been consulted so far as target acquisition was concerned, and over the selection of towns, industrial or military complexes to be destroyed and with which type of nuclear weapon, they have not been involved in the operational decision-making in respect of the launching of the weapons themselves.

This complete subjugation of NATO's strategy to the needs and interests of the United States, illustrated in the transition from 'massive retaliation' to 'flexible response', is at the root of the serious doubts about the credibility and usefulness of NATO's European nuclear strategy.

Firstly, the strategy of flexible response is nothing but an attempt to localize and therefore limit the risks involved in the use of nuclear weapons. General de Gaulle recognised this only too well.

Secondly, it presupposes the use of nuclear systems which will provoke retaliation fatal for Western Europe. These weapons therefore lack credibility as a means of defence.

Thirdly, a nuclear strike initiated from the soil of Western Europe will have the same consequences as would a strategic strike launched from outside Europe. In both cases the United States would have to decide whether or not it is worth engaging in nuclear war for the sake of Western Europe.

France's withdrawal from the military part of NATO followed that country's realization that NATO's nuclear strategy was only dictated by American interest. However, American nuclear weapons have played an important role in the US achieving political and military

[74]

dominance over the remaining NATO allies.

The public is becoming increasingly aware that those West European countries who directly confront the Warsaw Pact countries geographically and militarily face the highest risk in any conflict, which will inevitably take place on their territory. However, the decision whether or not to use nuclear weapons — a life or death decision for Western Europe — will be taken at a distance, in the United States, by people who may believe that they can survive and win a nuclear war. Taking decisions in a context so far removed from their consequences naturally increases the tendency to run political and military risks. Much more than the United States, Western Europe has for many years been exposed to the potential risks of miscalculations, of technical failures in safety precautions and of human failure due to stress. For American military leaders and politicians, a war in Europe would be a troublesome and problematic affair, but for the Europeans themselves it is a totally unacceptable risk. That is why a realistic security policy, which takes into account the specific European conditions of the two military blocs confronting each other, is the only way of avoiding war. To believe that one can prevent war by military means is both illusory and dangerous.

The piling up of nuclear weapons in Europe is pointless in political as well as in military terms. The mutual military threat will not just fade away because the arms race is stepped up by one side or the other. Accumulating nuclear weapons reduces opportunities of reaching a political agreement with the other side, especially if the military threat to use them lacks credibility. It is obvious that irrational military behaviour gives rise to doubts about the ability and willingness to solve political conflicts in a rational manner.

The mere existence of nuclear arsenals places the whole of Europe in danger of annihilation. The mere existence of this huge destructive nuclear potential represents a grave threat to security. Failure of control and safety mechanisms or mistaken judgements could easily transform Europe into a dead continent.

The existence of nuclear weapons in Europe is a contradiction in moral terms of any security policy. The attacker and the attacked will both suffer the same fate — the consequences will be equally shared.

It should not be forgotten that the effects of nuclear weapons will not stop at national borders. The demand for territorial integrity is therefore incompatible with the mere existence of these weapon systems, let alone their use. The situation is made even worse by the fact that the nuclear arms deployed in Western Europe — with the exception of France and Great Britain — are exclusively American. Neither governments nor parliaments of the countries involved have the right of veto against their use.

It is obvious that nuclear weapons cannot meet the defence requirements of Western Europe. Their use would inevitably lead to the destruction of what they are intended to defend. It is important to recognize that there are no formal dual decision-taking agreements between the USA and her NATO allies regarding the firing of these weapons. If it came to the point, the USA could order the launching of a nuclear strike without first obtaining the acquiescence of its NATO partners. To effect a first strike capability, the weapons need to be deployed early. The majority of American nuclear weapons in Europe are deployed near the 'front line'; it is estimated that about 5,000 nuclear warheads are deployed in West Germany alone. They are also deployed in Italy and Turkey, in close proximity to the Warsaw Pact countries. In the case of an armed conflict, these nuclear systems, which are vulnerable to conventional attacks, would have to be used very early or they would be lost. This is particularly true of the new intermediate-range systems which, if deployed, will actually threaten Soviet territory, thus becoming prime targets of any military action by the Warsaw Pact. This situation has several implications:

(a) the deployment of NATO's nuclear weapons is justified only if there is an intention to strike first;

(b) any conventional conflict between NATO and Warsaw Pact in Central Europe would pose a threat to these nuclear arms systems and would make their early use almost a certainty;

(c) there is absolutely no doubt that the Russians would strike back with nuclear weapons and turn Western Europe into a nuclear desert.

Forward-based deployment of nuclear weapons necessarily reduces the chance for conventional defence and involves the risk of nuclear escalation. The states of Western Europe are thus prisoners of the military doctrine of flexible response, yet this doctrine lacks credibility because the chances are that it would lead promptly to nuclear escalation. If one looks at the positions of nuclear arms depots in West Germany, it is evident that NATO could not recover from the slightest territorial loss. American nuclear depots would be exposed to direct attacks by the Warsaw Pact. Therefore it is questionable whether NATO's flexible response doctrine could provide a true choice between conventional or nuclear defence. It is probably limited to a choice between various nuclear weapons only, any of which would trigger a nuclear inferno and the total annihilation of Europe.

Regrettably, the mass media have done little to ensure that these interrelations are understood by the general public. The complex military technicalities involved facilitate the deception of parliamentarians and ministers as to the true consequences of NATO's military plans. In fact, the consequences of a nuclear first strike or first use would be devastating for Eastern and Western Europe alike. From a European point of view, they are incompatible with the requirements of a rational security policy.

It is instructive to compare this concept with the Warsaw Pact's political and military plans. It is generally known that nuclear weapons are not deployed on Warsaw Pact territories bordering on NATO territories.* Delivery vehicles that can be equipped with conventional as well as with nuclear charges have been deployed in East Germany and in Czechoslovakia but the nuclear warheads themselves have so far remained exclusively in the Soviet Union. Thus the situation of the East European countries could be compared with that of the Scandinavian NATO members who refuse to store or deploy nuclear weapons on their soil in peacetime.

In military terms, this means that the Warsaw Pact has greater latitude than NATO:
— in the event of a conventional war, Soviet nuclear arsenals would not be directly threatened. The Soviet Union therefore is not faced with NATO's 'use them or lose them' alternative;
— the renunciation of a first use of nuclear weapons is possible and plausible from a military point of view;
— in the event of escalation to nuclear war, flexibility of military action can be fully maintained.

This shows to what extent military plans and their political consequences are interrelated. The different modes of deployment in the two alliances are such that it is probable, if it came to the point, that NATO would be the first to cross the nuclear threshold.

The problem appears in a different light, however, when considered from an American point of view: that the use of nuclear weapons can be contained, territorially, qualitatively and quantitatively. In this

---

* Since the publication of this book in its original German version, it is believed that intermediate-range missiles have been deployed in Czechoslovakia and East Germany a counter to NATO's Cruise and Pershing II deployments.

[77]

case, a nuclear confrontation restricted to the European theatre of war would provide an opportunity to inflict heavy losses on the Warsaw Pact countries while passing the military burden to America's political allies, West Germany, France and Great Britain. Not more than 350,000 US troops would be directly exposed to danger. Perhaps strategic considerations like these may be encouraged — consciously or unconsciously — by the fact that nobody alive in America today has ever experienced a war in their own country, in contrast to those people of Eastern and Western Europe who have experienced the devastation of war twice in this century. The European and American experiences in those wars cannot be compared. Military losses apart, the Europeans experienced a full-scale war which affected social and industrial life and their recovery in the postwar period. Not having suffered in the same way, the United States was able to emerge from the Second World War as the dominant political, economic and military power in the Western hemisphere, if not the world. For these reasons it is understandable why America's attitude towards war in Europe is what it is and why its doctrine of flexible response has become NATO's.

The deployment of nuclear weapons in Western Europe near Warsaw Pact territories, and a doctrine which allows for a nuclear first strike, make military sense only on two conditions.

Firstly, that the US nuclear potential deployed in Europe must be used preventively before it is endangered by the enemy's conventional weapons.

Secondly, it can only be used for offensive purposes since it is totally inappropriate as a means of defence. Thus the US potential deployed in Europe is no longer a means of deterrence — it has become a means of waging war.

To all intents and purposes, the arms programme is geared to derive for military superiority. Retired Admiral Gene La Rocque, Director of the Center for Defense Information in Washington and an expert with a profound knowledge of Pentagon strategy concepts, has made statements that should make us pause to consider. According to La Rocque, the Americans assume that, like its two predecessors, the Third World War will be fought in Europe. He writes that US military planners are convinced that a war between the USA and the USSR will happen sooner or later — and that it will be a nuclear one.[11] Again and again the Pentagon argues that it is entirely up to the United States to determine which weapons should be issued to the American

Forces stationed in Western Europe, and how they should be used. After all, they contend, it is a matter of US soldiers and US weapons safeguarding Western Europe's security. Legally, this point of view is correct. The 1952 Forces Convention between the Federal Republic of Germany and the three Western powers (Convention on the Rights and Obligations of the Foreign Forces and their Members in the Federal Republic of Germany) gives the USA a free hand to deploy on West German territory whatever weapons and forces it deems necessary. The Convention does not contain any restrictions regarding the deployment of nuclear weapons.

The Supreme Commander of NATO's armed forces in Europe (at the time of writing, General Rogers) is at the same time simultaneously Supreme Commander of the US Armed Forces in Europe. When it comes to deciding whether or not nuclear weapons should be used, NATO's Supreme Commander is bound only by a vaguely worded duty to 'consult' with the Allies on whose territory nuclear war is to be waged 'if time permits'. An operation order from the President of the United States could launch American missiles totally independently of her NATO allies. As already mentioned, the European members of NATO participate in the top secret decision-making process which selects nuclear targets and the choice of the nuclear systems to be used for their destruction, but have nothing to do with decisions about the actual use of nuclear weapons: that remains in the hands of the Americans.

Admiral La Rocque, contradicting statements by the British Government, points out that European political and military leaders are not automatically a party to decisions on the use of nuclear weapons, nor do they have the power of veto over those decisions. The question arose in debates in the British Parliament, when the planned deployment of US Cruise missiles on British soil was being discussed. La Rocque wrote:

> I favour close cooperation within NATO and an effective defence for all NATO members but we must face facts. American nuclear weapons are American nuclear weapons, whether they are located in the United States, at sea, or in Europe. The American nuclear weapons in Europe, and those that are to come, are totally under the control of the US Government. They will be used only if and when the US Government decides to do so. . . . No prior understandings or arrangements about consultation will alter this fact.

[79]

No member of NATO has a veto power over American nuclear weapons.[12]

What this means is that West European states have given up an essential right of national sovereignty. But there is more to it than this. On 19 August 1981, *The Times* concluded that:

The single most striking feature of NATO's nuclear planning over the past thirty years is how few Europeans have been involved in it. The nuclear élite of Europe — those few politicians, civil servants, soldiers and academics who discuss and contribute to the formation of nuclear policy — is tiny. Right now, it probably numbers no more than 150, and some reckonings put the real inner circle as low as twenty.

The real implications of a nuclear war, a matter of life or death, are neither fully understood by the general public in Western Europe nor within its power to control. Nuclear strategy, the crucial issue of present-day military policy, is decided by people whose technical knowledge and intellectual competence can only be a matter of speculation. The majority of parliamentarians and members of West European governments are kept in ignorance of the facts necessary to evaluate nuclear strategies and the small circle of people who do have the requisite knowledge are not in a position to influence the American President or his military deputy in Europe.

Seen in this light, one may well question the common notion of a Soviet threat to the sovereignty of the West European states. It is equally dubious to conjure up the nightmare of 'nuclear blackmail' as an alternative to a freeze or a reduction in the existing nuclear arsenals. Unknown to the public, the sovereign rights of states, even of individuals, are being suppressed to meet the requirements of these policies.

The USA's 'victory is possible' plan, its 'first strike' mentality and the refusal to renounce a first use of nuclear weapons, have led to several fundamental problems, both with regard to national legislation in the USA and for its NATO partners, and to the laws and codes governing international behaviour.

According to US legislation, the planning and preparation of military aggression is prohibited but who is going to prosecute those politicians and military leaders who violate this law and plan the use of weapons of mass destruction; even against people and states who neither possess such weapons nor pose any sort of a military threat to the United States?

In almost all NATO countries, the right to life is guaranteed and an obligation not to break the peace is anchored in the Constitution. The extent to which present NATO military policies conflict with these basic rights is particularly evident in the Federal Republic of Germany. West German territory not only has the highest concentration of nuclear weapons but, because of the geographical location, it is also the obvious starting point for any military operation by NATO and must be considered a Combat Zone (CZ).

The preamble and Article 2.2 of West Germany's constitution (Basic Law) proclaim the right to live in peace and freedom. We have already outlined the ways in which political and military integration into NATO and the authority of US military units in the Federal Republic of Germany restrict sovereign rights. Article 24.2 states in unequivocal terms that any restriction of sovereign rights must be related to promoting 'a special and lasting order in Europe and between the peoples of the world'. Article 26.1 is even more explicit: it threatens with punishment any actions designed and intended to disturb the peaceful cooperation of peoples, specifically the preparation of a war of aggression, and declares such acts to be unconstitutional.

In this context, the following measures would seem to be controversial and constitutionally contestable:
— measures that do not exclude nuclear warfare on German soil but accept it as an integral part of present military doctrines;
— measures that incur a renunciation of sovereign rights and irresponsibly forego the right of veto and control over the use of nuclear weapons on German territory;
— measures that will allow the deployment of arms which are capable of nuclear first strikes;
— measures that endanger the population by tolerating the storage of large amounts of US weapons designed for chemical warfare.

It would be difficult to prove that the deployment of nuclear weapons on West German territory promotes peace. Why do we refuse to renounce the first use of nuclear weapons? Why do we not agree to the establishment of a nuclear-free zone? East Germany would be prepared to add the whole of its territory to a nuclear-free zone; neither let us forget that a nuclear warfare doctrine is inconsistent with many international treaties and agreements. The Hague Land Warfare Convention, for example, commits signatories to the

[81]

avoidance of civilian casualties in war and prohibits the use of all types of weapons of mass destruction; the United Nations Charter and the General Declaration on Human Rights in UN resolution 217A, of 10 December 1948, demand the protection of human life and peaceful cooperation between all peoples.

As we have seen, the West European governments are basically excluded from political and military decision-making on the use of nuclear weapons. This could lead to wrong political and military assessments and, consequently, to wrong decisions being made. But dangers may also arise as a result of technical breakdowns and human failure on the part of the people who make the decisions. Specialists give a high rating to the stress factor in those responsible for making and taking decisions on the use of nuclear weapons. This emerges from a report by Roger Molander, a former adviser on nuclear armament questions to several American presidents. He expected the office of the Nuclear Planning Group to be the last place in the world where he would meet people who lose their self-control. However, he experienced unrestrained fits of rage directed at government officials of other states, at staff officers, even at document files; in short, at anything. Molander had hoped that nuclear matters in the White House would be handled by people capable of rational thinking and self-control, even under pressure, but he soon saw that this was not the case.[13]

Molander's experiences corroborate the results of psychological research which show that political and military crises may cause symptoms of stress in the people in positions of responsibility, thus seriously limiting their capacity to make rational and appropriate decisions. Other psychological investigations have studied the effects of modern armament technology upon those persons involved in the launching of such weapons and the ways in which they can disociate themselves from the results of their action. Someone sitting in a command bunker and pressing the release button can watch the start and the trajectory of a nuclear missile but will not be confronted personally with the terrible effects of the nuclear explosion. The psychologists unanimously concluded that this considerably lowers psychological barriers to the use of weapons of mass destruction and that awareness of the consequences of actions decreases steadily. This led to the opinion that politicians and military leaders should view demonstration nuclear explosions and thus be made aware of their effects and experience their emotional impact. Another suggestion was

[82]

that the President of the United States should be compelled actually to shed blood with his own hands before triggering a world-wide nuclear catastrophe. This followed a report in the *International Herald Tribune* of 9 August 1982, of the findings of the International Society for Political Psychology as to how people could be tempted to use nuclear weapons:

It has long been feared that a president could be making his fateful decision while at a 'psychological distance' from the victims of a nuclear barrage; that he would be in a clean, air-conditioned room, surrounded by well-scrubbed aides, all talking in abstract terms about appropriate military responses in an international crisis, and that he might well push to the back of his mind the realization that hundreds of millions of people would be exterminated.[14]

Roger Fisher, Professor of Law at Harvard University, offered a simple suggestion to make the stakes more realistic. He suggested putting the code needed to fire nuclear weapons in a capsule and implanting it next to the heart of a volunteer who would carry a big butcher's knife as he accompanied the president everywhere. 'If the president ever wanted to fire nuclear weapons, he would first have to kill a human being with his own hands to get hold of the code.' It is not known to what extent these psychological opinions influence US nuclear policy, if at all, but it is undisputed that they do affect the assessment and evaluation of a threat, the capability to manage a crisis and attitudes towards the use of nuclear weapons.

The US Committee of Joint Chiefs of Staff must have come to similar conclusions. When the Nixon Administration was declining and signs of the president's growing psychic depression became alarming, the Joint Chiefs determined no longer to carry out his orders automatically if they could result in a nuclear war. At least, that is what Washington insiders said.

But those times of reason have passed. Nuclear strategic notions of victory have obviously supplanted rational considerations and caution. Nobody in today's US top military establishment seems to question the statements and decisions of their inexperienced president. But even if the decisions are not made by people like Reagan or Weinberger, they will always be American decisions and will always pursue objectives of US policy. All governments involved must take this into account. They must see to it that relations between United States and the other members of NATO are not dominated by American interests. It is their duty to establish political, economic and military cooperation on the basis of equality between all members of NATO.

NATO's two-track decision — an attempt to shift the strategic nuclear risk

When in 1962 the Soviet Union started to deploy intermediate-range missiles in Cuba which were capable of reaching American territory within minutes, the world was on the brink of a nuclear world war. When in 1983 the United States deployed its missiles on the Soviet Union's doorstep (from where they would take between six and ten minutes to hit the Kremlin or the Soviet Defence Ministry), a comparable situation arose. The action has provoked an increase in tension between NATO and Warsaw Pact countries and especially between the two super-powers. Nevertheless many politicians, military men and political scientists believe, or at least claim, that stepping up armament is the only suitable response to the new Soviet intermediate-range ballistic missiles. This idea has been widely publicized by the media. Almost nobody is willing to question whether it is correct. So-called 'authorities' voice their opinions and offer to do the thinking for all of us. After all, it was Henry Kissinger, former Secretary of State and presidential adviser for many years, who claimed that Western Europe could be politically and militarily 'blackmailed' by the Soviet SS-20 intermediate-range ballistic missiles.

Blackmail pre-supposes a unilateral advantage: someone holds the gun — the victim has to pay. Let us consider in more detail what this Russian 'gun' — the SS-20 — is all about. This ballistic missile is replacing the obsolete Soviet intermediate-range missiles SS-4 and SS-5, which have been directed at Western Europe since the beginning of the 1960s. It is true that the SS-20 is both more accurate and more mobile than its predecessors but this does not in any way change the Soviet Union's capability to bomb Europe into oblivion. It has had this capability since the 1960s but Western Europe has not been susceptible to political or military blackmail. The Soviet Union did not even attempt to put it to the test. This is certainly not due to the fact that until recently American has had a superiority of strategic nuclear weapons. President Kennedy's reaction at the time of the Cuban crisis showed that the consequences of a nuclear war were as unacceptable to

[84]

both sides then as they are today. At the beginning of the 1960s, the United States had a superiority of nuclear weapons and delivery vehicles but this was correctly assessed to be politically and militarily irrelevant. The Soviet missiles which threaten *Western* Europe are matched by US missiles and other nuclear devices threatening *Eastern* Europe. After all, the number of nuclear weapons deployed in West Germany alone is estimated to be 4,000 to 5,000. The majority are designed to be used against East Germany, Czechoslovakia and Poland, and perhaps Hungary and the Western part of the USSR as well. In other words, NATO is holding a 'gun' and to talk about blackmail does not make sense.

To assess the problem of mutual threat, it is necessary to consider in more detail the methods of calculation used by representatives of NATO and of the American Administration. They refer selectively to land-based intermediate-range ballistic missiles in order to prove NATO's inferiority and show how far it has to 'catch up'. A brochure entitled *Aspects of Peace Policy*, published by the West German government, claims that the Soviet Union's 600 intermediate-range missiles with approximately 1,000 warheads are opposed by no more than 18 French missiles. The ratio is therefore 50:1 in favour of the Soviet Union. Let us be consistent, follow this argument through and compare the sea-based nuclear systems. On page 179 of *SIPRI Yearbook 1980* there is a list of 20 sea-based Soviet intermediate-range missiles and 224 Western sea-based missiles with a total of 1,072 warheads:

80 French SLBM	with 80 warheads
64 British Polaris SLBM	with 192 warheads
80 American Poseidon SLBM	with 800 warheads

If one follows the same selective method of counting sea-based intermediate-range missiles as used for the SS-20s, the Soviet Union has every reason to become frightened and to start 'catching up', because the ratio is now 1:11 to their disadvantage in terms of submarine missiles and 1:54 in terms of warheads.

The absurdity of these selective assessments is clear. With regard to intermediate-range missiles an approximate parity has been reached and there is no necessity at all to continue arming. The Soviet Union favours land-based missiles because it has only a few ice-free ports; geographical circumstances have similarly influenced NATO countries to favour deploying at sea. This sort of selective comparison is not, however, restricted to intermediate-range systems. It is also applied to strategic components in order to fabricate a threat to America's land-based intercontinental ballistic missiles. Although Soviet land-based missiles are as vulnerable to US attack as vice versa, the USA claim that a unilateral threat exists which has necessitated the development of the first strike MX missile system.

Let us just consider the five American Poseidon submarines that have been allocated to NATO and are explicitly described as 'theatre nuclear forces'. They alone have at least 800 warheads. This potential is sufficient to counter the Soviet Union's intermediate-range missiles if range, penetration capability and survival capacity are compared and if their military function is defined as non-strategic. Until their response to the deployment of Cruise and Pershing II in late 1983 and early 1984 respectively, the Soviet Union had no nuclear weapons deployed in Czechoslovakia, East Germany or Poland.

These countries are facing a massive American and British and an increasing French nuclear threat. If they were not to rely on Soviet guarantees of protection, they would be forced either to develop their own nuclear weapons or — analogous to West Germany — ask the Soviet Union to deploy their nuclear weapons on East European territory. The fact that this step has now been taken represents a move to neutralize the effect of America's deployments; the American threat arising from the presence of nuclear arms in West Germany and Italy can only be neutralized by missiles that can directly threaten the USA. Since Cuba would probably not be willing to offer its territory for this kind of undertaking, use might have to be made of East German, Polish and Czech ships besides those of the Russians cruising close to American territorial waters and carrying short-range Soviet missiles for attacks against US coastal cities. In view of the threat represented by US nuclear arms in West European countries, it is surprising that the East European countries have not so far expressed their own security interests more firmly.

The outcome of this analysis is that, in the field of intermediate-range nuclear weapons, a mutual threat exists but the potential for unilateral blackmail does not. Why then do new missiles that can reach the USSR have to be deployed in Western Europe? The United States has made it clear that it is striving for military superiority over the Soviet Union. This intention is expressed in the deployment of new missiles that can reach Moscow within minutes and are capable of destroying any given target with the utmost precision. The 'time factor' will favour the Americans in any race for strategic advantages. Moreover, the fact that American missiles are deployed far from American territory may encourage the illusion that a counter-strike would be directed exclusively at the deployment sites of the missiles and not at US towns or at US political and military command centres. They are weapons designed to 'decapitate' the state and the armed forces of the USSR. In this context they are military rather than political weapons. Nevertheless, they still constitute a means by which mass destruction can result from the holocaust of a nuclear exchange.

Even if one believes that security can be achieved by this kind of risky nuclear threat, the consequences need to be carefully considered. There is no doubt that the Soviet Union possesses a wide range of measures which could neutralize any unilateral increase in Western 'security due to military superiority'. The inevitable result would be a high-level nuclear confrontation which would lead to a loss of, rather than a gain in security for both sides. The well-known peace researcher Carl Friedrich von Weizsäcker and several British politicians have developed the idea of sea-based missiles as an alternative to the deployment of Pershing IIs and Cruise missiles in five West European countries. If the Soviet Union and its allies were to take up this idea, for example, they would deploy sea-based intermediate-range ballistic missiles near the US coast. The military advantage that this would not expose densely-populated areas to the danger of a retaliatory strike against deployment sites — one of the main arguments of the advocates of sea-based deployment — would in this case go to the Soviet Union. Another possibility is the deployment of Soviet SS-20 missiles in areas of Soviet territory from which they could reach the United States; or the Soviet Union could deploy short-range nuclear missiles in Eastern European countries. These are just a few possibilities. The Russians could also quickly implement measures against 'decapitating blows', such as the establishment of flying or land-mobile command centres and the mobile deployment of strategic ballistic missiles.

Apart from any military and political reservations about the deployment of new US intermediate-range ballistic missiles in Western Europe, technology as a source of danger should not be forgotten. In a well-documented study, *Armaments and Peace*, Alfred Mechtersheimer correctly points out that fears of nuclear weapons being launched as the result of a technical fault are well-founded. He suggests that the machinery of nuclear destruction does not have to be

[87]

set into motion by a complicated process; it is in a state of permanent readiness. An insignificant technical failure could start a catastrophe. Peace and nuclear war are separated only by a few minutes.[15] Pershing II missiles take only that time to get from West German territory to the Kremlin, which is not long enough to correct any possible technical or human failure. It also means that all suggestions — such as those made by US Senators Cranston and Jackson or by President Reagan himself — of minimizing dangers resulting from computer breakdowns or human and technical failures by establishing control groups in both capitals and other measures, are rendered useless. The new intermediate-range missiles represent the surest means of testing the limits of technical and human control capability — and at the highest possible level of risk.

The danger of technical and human failure is considerably enhanced by first-strike ambitions and 'nuclear victory' doctrines because the enemy will conclude that it must launch its missiles while those of the opposite side are on their way (launch on warning). We know of several American cases of computer failure and of misinterpretations of radar signals caused by flocks of wild geese or meteorites which led to preparations for launching strategic weapons. Fortunately, there has always been sufficient time to recognize the error and stop launching preparations. It would be idle to speculate about the efficiency of Soviet computers or the competence of the commanders of strategic missiles units when US missiles take only six minutes to reach their targets. There will be no time to correct decisions or to use the red telephone (hot line) — there will just be time to supervise the pre-programmed launching procedures. What price Western Europe then!

In his study, A. Mechtersheimer suggests that NATO's two -track decision is one that will step up the arms race. If one assumes that it was made on a rational basis, it is unlikely that any reduction in the Soviet's potential would cause that decision to be reversed. Mechtersheimer believes that the intention to deploy missiles could only be given up if the conceptual trends of American strategy were to be reversed and, since that will not happen, the INF negotiations at Geneva are merely meant to weaken political resistance against deployment at home.[16]

As early as May 1978, the US Army announced its intention to deploy a brigade equipped with Pershing II missiles in West Germany —eighteen months before SS-20s were held to be responsible for NATO's decision to step up the arms race. One brigade is made up of three battalions with thirty-six missiles each — a total of 108 Pershing II missiles. Eight months later, in February 1979, the American armaments company Martin received a 360 million dollar contract to produce Pershing IIs. The company made sub-contracts with Bendix Corporation, Goodyear, Hercules and Singer-Kearfott. From the start, it is easy to see that the United States used the two-track decision as a reason for deployment, while carrying on arms control negotiations with the USSR; more for appearances sake than anything else. Some West European governments, and certainly a great majority of the general public, believed that the deployment was actually related to the outcome of the negotiations. An editorial in the *Frankfurter Allgemeine Zeitung* established that there was a discrepancy between the real objectives of US armament policy and the expectations of the West Europeans. The zero option proposed by the United States was indeed an empty gesture. Because of the relative parity already existing, the proposal that the USSR should abandon its SS-20 programme and dismantle those already deployed in return for a cancellation of America's planned deployments of Cruise and Pershing II was not militarily realistic. While it might have been meant to mollify Western public opinion, it ensured that there would be a negative result to the negotiations currently under way. Can we really believe that the United States is seriously interested in finding ways of avoiding an arms race in the field of intermediate-range weapons? It would appear that she is much more interested in deploying her 572 intermediate-range missiles which can threaten the Soviet Union than in removing Soviet intermediate-range missiles which cannot threaten the USA. It is a matter of concern that West European governments ignore this American approach, tending to take a more benign view of Reagan's Administration, in contrast to the more critical voices heard in the United States itself. This is why the attitude of the present Administration is often assumed, wrongly, to represent the 'point of view of all Americans' and anyone who speaks out against it is branded as being anti-American. Certainly, a country whose economic and financial policies have been damaging to itself and other countries can hardly be said to have found a solution to our security problems.

According to a documentary report of the Washington Center for Defense Information, the United States intends to increase the number of its strategic warheads from 10,000 to 27,000 by the end of the decade. If one takes into account that the deployment of Cruise missiles and Pershing II, not only both in Western Europe and also in the Far East, is part of the encirclement of the USSR, then these measures are designed not so much to deter, but more to threaten to inflict unacceptable damage on Soviet towns and industrial areas. A few hundred strategic nuclear weapons would be sufficient for that purpose and would create the conditions for nuclear war by which every likely target can be covered by several nuclear weapons, with Europe as the central combat zone. The Pentagon guideline document, 'Air–Land–Battle–2000', and the armed forces' manual FM100-5, if implemented, could make a nuclear war not more winnable but more likely.

Only by analysing the US deployment plans for Western Europe do the dangers become apparent. It could involve the use of military means to overcome political and economic resistance by Western Europe to a policy of confrontation with Eastern Europe. The new US intermediate-range missiles represent the cornerstone of US attempts to attain weapon superiority in Europe. They are intended to change radically the military strategic balance of forces and in doing so will create a qualitatively new situation in Europe. They have a destabilizing effect and increase the feeling of mutual threat. To the Soviet Union, the strategic threat is unmistakable. The deployment of intermediate-range weapons as part of the encirclement of the USSR has removed all lingering doubts about the United States' intentions. They see Washington indulging in a verbal strong man act of threatening the USSR with war and annihilation. But what will be the benefit for the West Europeans, Americans, Russians or any other nation from this? What will be gained if these arms systems are not only deployed but actually used?

We know the argument that the arms race is necessary to defend our social and political system which is threatened by Eastern Europe but are intermediate-range nuclear weapons suitable for this purpose? What would remain of our Western system if they were really to be used? Can we regard the survival of a few people in bunkers as a true expression of our notions of freedom and democracy? Can the term 'survival' be so limited that it applies only to the physical survival of a chosen few? Nuclear intermediate-range weapons are totally inappropriate as a means of maintaining our social and political order and our idea of human values. In view of the actual consequences of a nuclear war, the 'red or dead' alternative does not even arise.

Dimensions of destruction in the case of a nuclear exchange on a 'European Theatre of War'

We should like once again to quote Admiral La Rocque's evaluation of the situation:

> If orders come from the President of the United States to use the 7,000 plus nuclear weapons in Europe, and if the orders get through to the field commanders, the systematic destruction of Europe will begin. On the NATO side alone there could be:
> — thousands of nuclear artillery shells fired against the Soviet ground forces;
> — hundreds of atomic demolition mines exploded inside NATO territory to destroy bridges and impede lines of communications;
> — hundreds of Pershing II and Cruise missiles launched against pre-selected targets in the USSR and Eastern Europe;
> — over a thousand NATO aircraft armed with nuclear weapons ready for launching. (Twelve hundred more aircraft will be flown to Europe in the first week of fighting from the US.);
> — hundreds of Navy carrier planes equipped with nuclear weapons will launch them against maritime targets on the flanks of NATO;
> — US missile submarines committed to NATO will fire nearly 500 nuclear weapons against enemy targets in Europe.
> In all, there could be some 8,000 to 10,000 nuclear explosions in the European theatre initiated by NATO alone.
> War plans call for the destruction of every Soviet and Warsaw Pact Division which could threaten NATO forces. . . .
> Assuming the Soviets respond in kind, they would add another 5,000–6,000 nuclear explosions in Europe. The total effect of exploding over 15,000 nuclear weapons in a short period of time is impossible to measure. In all the history of nuclear weapons, never has there been more than one nuclear weapon exploded at a time. . . .
> Some measure of the effectiveness can be gleaned from the fact that the fire power in just one of the NATO nuclear missile submarines exceeds the total fire power from all explosives used in World War II. We also know that one small 13 kiloton bomb exploded over Hiroshima killed 100,000 people.
> American estimates given at Congress hearings reckon that 100 million Europeans could die in a nuclear war in Europe.[17]

It is open to question whether these estimates are not too low. In any case, victims would not die in the usual sense of the word. They would perish in extreme pain, burn, choke or bleed to death or would die of hunger and thirst. An area which has supported hundreds of millions of people would become uninhabitable and Europe would cease to exist as a centre of human civilization. That is why the *American* Admiral La Rocque comes to the conclusion — a conclusion which others in Europe should also have arrived at — that: 'Many options are open to us in NATO and in the Warsaw Pact to reduce the risk of war. But the initiatives for change must come from those countries in the nuclear theatre. Nuclear war in Europe is too important to be left to foreign decisions.'[18] In reality, the effects of even a regional use of nuclear weapons cannot be assessed. They would be much greater if a nuclear exchange should take on global dimensions, which is possible. There would follow the destruction of the biosphere, the destruction of the very means necessary to support life on this planet and world-wide contamination from radiation. There is no such thing as a 'humane' nuclear war directed against 'military targets' while 'sparing' the civil population. Harry S. Truman justified the atom bomb on the grounds that it was used against military targets but the majority of the 100,000 people killed by the comparatively small 13 kiloton bomb were civilians. The ratio between military and civilian dead in wars since 1914 is worth noting:

War	Dead soldiers		Dead civilians
First World War 1914–1918	20	:	1
Second World War 1939–1945	1	:	1
Korean War 1950–53	1	:	5
Vietnam War 1961–1975	1	:	20

From a military point of view a nuclear war in Europe would mean that:
— the use of nuclear weapons could not be limited to military targets;
— in the case of an intensive nuclear combat, it would be impossible adequately to protect the civilian population;
— the annihilation of Europe would be total. Even those who survived the war would die of the after-effects.

[92]

Commonsense demands that a nuclear war must never happen — either in Europe or in any other part of the world! Prevention is the only protection from the consequences of a war.

Thomas K. Jones, previously an employee of the huge armament firm of Boeing and now in the Pentagon as Deputy Under Secretary responsible for research and technology in the field of strategic and tactical nuclear weapons, is also concerned with civil defence. He has attempted to justify the dangerous nuclear war-game and attitude towards a military solution represented by present US policy. His recipe for survival is extremely simple: 'Dig a hole in the ground, cover it with a few doors taken off their hinges and shovel 90 centimetres of dirt upon them'. Thus a nuclear war becomes a child's game that can be won — and survived — provided that there are plenty of shovels. Jones continues: 'After only one day you can leave your shelter and fetch water. In two years at the latest the whole country will have completely recovered from the effects'.[19]

Jones is not the only person holding these views. Roger Molander, former strategy expert of the US National Security Council (NSC), describes meeting a Pentagon naval officer who thought that the consequences of a nuclear war were unduly exaggerated. According to him, a nuclear war would not bring about the end of the world. It would probably kill only about 500 million people and, within one generation, genetic sciences would make it possible to immunise people against radiation.[20]

A British Government 'information' pamphlet, optimistically entitled *Protect and Survive*, offers similar advice. People are told to pile up sandbags and books around a table, thus creating a miniature cave to withstand the radiation, the fire and windstorms. Smart business-men have established a 'survival industry' on this basis. It is not that we object to their making a profit out of it, but to the blind ignorance which believes that a nuclear war can be waged and survived.

Responsible scientists, and above all prominent medical experts, have countered these ideas with a realistic picture of the consequences of a nuclear strike. There is a particularly impressive description of the effects of a nuclear explosion over New York — it could just as well be Hamburg, London or Paris — in Jonathan Schell's book *The Fate of the Earth*. The dropping of one megaton bomb, that is one with sixty times the explosive force of the Hiroshima bomb, is vividly described. Exploding about 2,500 metres above the Empire State building in New York, it will destroy or raze almost every building between

Battery Park and 125th Street; that is, within a radius of seven kilo-metres or over an area of roughly 160 square kilometres. It will cause extensive damage to buildings between the northern end of Staten Island and George Washington Bridge, that is, over an area of 500 square kilometres. People and debris will be thrown into the air and blown away by the shock wave. Within a radius of 160 square kilometres, walls, roofs and ceilings will tumble if they have not already been destroyed. People and furniture will be thrown into the streets. (In technical terms, this zone will be exposed to overpressures of at least 0.35 kilogrammes per square centimetre. By 'overpressure' we mean pressures exceeding normal atmospheric pressure.) Up to sixteen kilometres around ground-zero, the shock wave will whirl broken panes of glass and other sharp-edged objects through the air at high velocities, inevitably causing death or serious injury to those in the waves. People inside the buildings will be blasted into the streets with all the debris, and those who are outside will be buried under the rubble. The resulting windstorm will reach a velocity of 650 km/h up to three kilometres from ground zero and it will still be 300 km/h at a distance of six kilometres. In the meantime, the fireball will have expanded to a diameter of more than 1.5 kilometres and risen to a height of more than ten kilometres. The town below will be exposed to its heat wave for about ten seconds. The people who are outside will probably die of third-degree burns within a radius of fifteen kilometres around ground-zero. Those nearer to the centre of the explosion will be charred on the spot. From Greenwich Village to Central Park in New York City, the heat will be so intense that metals and glass will melt. Everything inflammable within a radius of fifteen kilometres from ground-zero will burst into flames so that a total area of 670 square kilometres may be exposed to intensive conflagration . . . the fireball will emit a glaring white light for about thirty seconds. Simul-taneously, the scorching heat will set alight everything that is inflammable and melt windows, cars, lamp posts — in short, anything made of metal or glass. People in the street will be turned instantly into human torches and will be charred in a matter of seconds. Against this horrifying background, all the scenes of agonizing death that took place in Hiroshima will be repeated, with the difference that not 100,000 but several millions of people will be affected. The citizens of New York will be burnt, crushed or killed by radiation in the same way that the inhabitants of Hiroshima were eradicated. The city and its population will be turned into a huge smouldering heap of rubble.

[94]

There might be some survivors in areas peripheral to the centre of the explosion, but the ensuing conflagration will force them either to abandon their relatives and others unable to flee, or to perish with them.[21]

Apart from the problem of survival, the question remains as to whether it will be possible to obtain any medical assistance. Physicians from all over the world have no doubts about the effects of the explosion. They have shown convincingly that those who believe there can be any survival are being completely unrealistic. Six weeks after the announcement of NATO's decision to step up armaments, in December 1979, the Federal Republic of Germany, the state with the highest nuclear density, introduced an obligatory course in disaster medicine for all medical practitioners, to be supervised by military medical personnel. This type of course is legally required by the Gesetz zur Anpassung des Gesundheitswesens an besondere Anforderungen des Verteidigungsfalles (Law on the Adaptability of the Public Health Service to the Special Requirements of a Case of Defence). 'Case of Defence' means in case of war or, more precisely, nuclear war in Europe. But what *are* the chances of receiving medical aid after a nuclear war? Will it be possible to help the people who have survived the explosion, the fire and the radiation? A nuclear war in Europe would be in no way comparable to the destruction of the two cities of Hiroshima and Nagasaki where transport, supply and communication structures remained basically intact. The use of nuclear weapons in Europe will certainly result in the devastation of large areas and the destruction of economic and administrative structures. There will be numerous specific after-effects which will limit the capacity of medical aid and care in completely new ways. Therefore we must differentiate between the primary, direct effects of a nuclear explosion and the secondary, indirect effects which will be no less grave.

It is usual to describe the power of nuclear weapons by comparing their explosive force with that of the conventional explosive trinitrotoluol (TNT). This approach is misleading, however, because nuclear weapons do not work only through their explosive force. At the time of explosion, fast neutron radiation is emitted, combined with gamma rays which are partly a reaction to the neutron radiation. The atomic fission of a nucleus produces neutrons which collide with surrounding matter like tiny projectiles. Gamma rays, on the other hand, are electro-magnetic rays, comparable to X-rays. Other electro-magnetic rays in the visible spectrum will be released in the form of the flash and fireball of a nuclear explosion as well as in heat radiation, which is part of the infra-red spectrum of electro-magnetic radiation. Immediately after the setting-off of an atomic weapon, the temperature in the centre of the explosion will reach several million degrees centigrade. An explosive force of 1 million tons of TNT (one megaton) will produce a fireball with a diameter of more than two kilometres. It will be four times as bright as the midday sun at a distance of eight kilometres. The heat radiation emitted by the fireball will be lethal up to a distance of eleven kilometres. That is only the beginning. The shock wave of the tremendous explosion will follow immediately, travelling at an initial speed several times faster than the speed of sound. In the case of a one megaton bomb, the shock wave will destroy buildings within a radius of seven kilometres. This will be followed for several seconds by a gust of wind reaching velocities of several hundred km/h, much more than the strongest hurricane we know. This explains why the TNT detonation equivalent covers only one of several characteristics of a nuclear explosion. And it is not necessarily the one with the greatest, most widely ranging effects. For instance, the explosive force of nuclear weapons with 'enhanced radiation', commonly known as neutron bombs, is much smaller than that of the neutron radiation which represents about 80 per cent of the energy released by the explosion.

In addition to these effects, every nuclear explosion produces radioactive fall-out, which consists of the radioactive fission products of the bomb itself and of matter that has become radioactively contaminated by the nuclear explosion. The amount of fall-out depends largely on the height of the explosion, that is, on whether the fireball touches the earth or not. Part of the radioactive fall-out will descend to earth shortly after the explosion and near the place of the detonation. The rest will be hurled into the upper layers of the atmosphere and will be spread all around the globe over a period of months or even years. The extent to which the highly radioactive 'close-in fall-out' spreads depends on the weather conditions, but above all on the direction and velocity of the wind.

A nuclear weapon with a TNT detonation equivalent of approximately sixty megatons was tested in 1961 in the Soviet Union. According to estimates published in *SIPRI Yearbook 1980*, the nuclear powers currently possess about 120 nuclear weapons with capabilities of five, nine, fifteen and twenty megatons. A large majority of the existing strategic nuclear weapons probably have explosive forces of approximately one megaton, the equivalent of which in conventional explosive TNT would fill 67,000 goods wagons. This would make a freight train which would stretch from Hamburg to Frankfurt in West Germany (about 600 km.). In contrast, the bombs dropped on Hiroshima and Nagasaki were mere toys. Their explosive force was between thirteen and twenty kilotons of TNT, that is, not much more than 1 per cent of the force of a one-megaton bomb today. Yet the Hiroshima bomb killed 75,000 people immediately and injured another 100,000 people out of a total population of 245,000. Ninety per cent of the buildings of the town were destroyed. Thirty of the 150 medical doctors and 126 of the 1,780 nurses of the town survived and were able to give medical assistance. Imagine the consequences of a one-megaton explosion! Direct and indirect radiation, thermic radiation and the shock wave of the explosion would create an indescribable inferno. According to American estimates, a one-megaton bomb dropped on Detroit would result in 470,000 people dead and 630,000 seriously injured. Because of the higher population density, the same kind of explosion over Leningrad would result in 890,000 dead and 1.26 million seriously injured. Only one such bomb would kill more American people than the United States lost during the whole of the Second World War.

But we are not talking about *one* bomb or *one* town. NATO and the Soviet Union have approximately 15,000 nuclear warheads designed solely for use in the European theatre of war. (The Soviet Union's share is estimated to be about 6,000.) Many are in the megaton range; the majority are smaller. For instance, the US forces' manuals FM100-5 and FM101-31 suggest stopping an armoured thrust by the Russians with a salvo of fifty nuclear grenades. Undoubtedly, Soviet forces would retaliate with nuclear arms, perhaps with fifty, probably with more. Large areas would be devastated and radioactively contaminated. Electricity, transport, supply and communication systems would break down completely. Casualties would number not hundreds but hundreds of thousands. Hospitals would be destroyed, medical doctors and nurses killed or wounded, medical supplies would soon run out and to transport the wounded to hospital would be virtually impossible. It would be equally impossible to render medical assistance in such chaotic situations for the following reasons:

(a) several of the effects of a nuclear explosion — from severe burns to radiation injuries — cannot be treated successfully even in fully functioning medical centres. They would undoubtedly be fatal;

[97]

(b) in the case of a nuclear attack, medical capacities would enable assistance to be given only to a minute fraction of the overall number of casualties. This means that aid would only be given selectively;

(c) treating radiation in a contaminated area would most certainly be lethal for the helpers. In those places where help would be required most urgently, nobody would be able to rescue and evacuate the injured;

(d) all rescue operations would be rendered useless in view of the wide-spread long-term effects of atomic explosions. Food and water would be contaminated. After stored supplies were used up, there would at best be only radioactive water, contaminated plants, fruit and cattle.

Professor Messerschmidt, a medical officer in the West German Bundeswehr, in his book *Medical Procedures in a Nuclear Disaster*, advises classifying the wounded into four groups; some injured people will receive no medical assistance at all. Messerschmidt openly admits:

> We cannot exclude the fact that situations may arise in which the wounded and the victims of radiation would have to be treated without any outside help. There will be so many of them awaiting treatment that the demands on emergency hospitals would be several times higher than their capacities. Treatment would have to be started without drugs and wound dressing materials, and food and drinking water would soon be used up. It would be a situation unparalleled in history, not only because of the completely new biological effects of these weapons but also because of the inconceivable dimensions of the collapse of any supply system.[22]

No further comment is necessary.

The people who experienced the massive bombings of the Second World War, and survived the turmoil of the whining and detonating bombs in air raid shelters and bunkers, could leave their shelters after the attacks were over. They could come up into the open air, drink water, eat food and search for their relatives. This knowledge gave them courage and strength amidst the chaos of bombs exploding all round them. In a nuclear war there will be no liberating and safe 'outside'. For the few people who might find protection in shelters and thus survive the attack, the outside world will be 'off limits'; there will only be contaminated air, contaminated soil and contaminated water. Smart businessmen are making high profits from the anxiety business. Using the slogan 'Survive!', they are selling prefabricated shelters, speculating with real estate in remote areas and selling firearms for 'defence' against other survivors looking for help. On behalf of the Swiss Government, the Nestlé Company is selling 'pemmican for the third millenium' — canned food for survival: a sweetened variety for breakfast and a salted one for main dishes. But what will happen when the cans are empty, the water used up and the air filters jammed with radioactive particles while the outside world is still contaminated? The inhabitants of Rongelap, a Pacific island contaminated by American nuclear tests, have had to give up any hopes of resettlement even after decades because the island is still radioactive. The same fate awaits Europe!

It is simply impossible to protect the population adequately from the effects of nuclear war. That is why more and more responsible scientists are rejecting a policy that regards nuclear war as acceptable and winnable. American medical doctors in the association Physicians for Social Responsibility have therefore appealed to the general public, to the political representatives of the United States and the USSR and to physicians in both countries to assess the consequences of a nuclear war more realistically; to show more responsibility in political behaviour. They emphasize that there will be no winner in a nuclear war. The radioactive fall-out will spread all around the world and will contaminate most of the globe for several generations. The atmospheric effects will severely damage all living beings. Therefore, the American physicians call for the protection of humanity:
— by a reduction in existing international tensions;
— by a prohibition on the use of all kinds of nuclear weapons;
— by a recognition of the dangers inherent in the existing huge nuclear arsenals and for a start to be made on their dismantling.[23]

Economic and social consequences of nuclear armament

A new Pentagon guideline document calls for the US armed forces to eliminate the military and political power structures of the Soviet Union and its satellites and to destroy their nuclear and conventional armed forces and industries essential to their military viability. This makes heavy demands on the capacities of the US armed forces. In the context of a strategy of global confrontation, these demands set new standards for nuclear and conventional armament. Nuclear armament is by no means as 'inexpensive' as some people would have us

[99]

believe. On the contrary, today's expenditure on arms sets new levels for armaments over the entire military spectrum. In other words, it is not a choice between nuclear *or* conventional, it is a matter of nuclear *and* conventional armament. This means that the economic and social consequences of nuclear armament must be considered in relation to all other fields of military expenditure; it cannot be taken out of context. The same applies to the connection between nuclear armament and military strategies. In the light of modern armament finances, the United States' present military programme is characterized:

firstly, by its unparalleled dimensions and by a large rate of increase in military expenditure;

secondly, by increased expenditure for arms purchases while the number of troops remains relatively steady; and

thirdly, by an orientation towards a rapid increase in military research and development, which are considered to be major factors in achieving military and technological superiority.

The consequences are not confined to the armament industry. Apart from revolutionary developments in this industry and its scientific and technological basis, military budgets and armament programmes will inevitably exert a stronger influence on the overall development of the US economy in the future. But there is even more to it; since the Second World War the United States has developed such a huge and efficient arms industry that it has easily become the world's largest and most important exporter of arms. It also plays a far larger part in the arms production of Western industrial countries — the majority of them members of NATO — than in their overall industrial output. For instance, the United States produces approximately 75 per cent of all missiles technology manufactured in NATO countries, approximately 60 per cent of the naval vessels and about half of all artillery and infantry weapons. 'One-way preferences' are typical of American policies, meaning that US military technology can be freely imported into all the other NATO countries, while arms exports from Europe to the United States are largely excluded. By introducing the Speciality Metal Clause, prohibiting the import of armament products, the Senate and House of Representatives have given a free hand to those US firms which had been fighting for the market share of the European firms in the armaments industry. Finally, it should be made clear that NATO members have to contribute financially to the US Pershings and Cruise missiles deployed in Western Europe, over which they will have no control.

The overall effects of nuclear armament are thus felt not only by the United States and the other nuclear arms producers, France and the United Kingdom, but also by all member states of NATO. The consequences are political as well as economic. Let us consider them in detail.

The economic and political impact of President Reagan's armament policy is reflected in the increasing proportion of the Federal budget devoted to military expenditure. It is to increase from 22.9 per cent in the 1980 fiscal year to 37.2 per cent in the 1987 fiscal year. In view of the growing deficit of the US annual budgets, several lobby groups are worried because their own economic interests have been impaired by the preferential treatment accorded to the arms industry. Speaker O'Neill complained that President Reagan was out of touch with reality and obviously did not understand what the consequences of this programme would be for the American nation. Senator D. Pryor pointed out that the armament companies were besieging Capitol Hill. In the expectation of higher profits, they were demanding increased expenditure under the pretext of Soviet superiority. The Senator quite correctly asked whether their motivation was in fact the safeguarding of the nation's defence or merely the desire for profits.

The list of expenditures for strategic arms systems is considerable. In October 1981, 180 billion dollars were made available for the modernization of strategic forces. Part of it will be spent as follows:

- 42 billion dollars for the development and production of sea-based missiles;
- 34 billion dollars for the production of land-based MX missiles;
- 63 billion dollars for the modernization of the B-52 bomber; for the production of the new B-1B and of the 'invisible' stealth bomber;
- 18 billion dollars for new control, command and communications systems.

However, this planned expenditure will most certainly not correspond to the actual prices to be paid. It is well-known that the prices of armaments rise quickly. An investigation by a US Congressional Committee showed that the prices of major arms systems had increased by 31 per cent in 1969 and by 190 per cent (!) in June 1981. This is much higher than the general rate of increase in the prices of industrial products and very much higher than the inflation rate. These price increases may well be a cause of inflation, rather than its result. The extremely high profit margins of the armament industry, considerably above the normal level, have led to increased investment in this field. Experts from Columbia University have established that as early as 1977 the armament industry's share of new investments had reached approximately 46 per cent. If nearly half of the new investments in any country are made in armament industries, it is logical to expect that its economy and its power to compete internationally will be negatively affected. The fact that there is prosperity in some areas does not compensate for an overall deficit in the economy. It will only promote disproportional developments in the future instead of reducing them. Therefore the statement that armament creates jobs is not true.

Every citizen knows that expenditure on armaments reflects a loss in the amount spent on social programmes. Scientific analyses confirm this and also show that the billions of dollars spent on armaments could more sensibly be used to create new jobs. One billion dollars invested in the armaments industry creates 75,710 new jobs; invested otherwise, the same amount could create 187,300 new jobs in education, 138,900 in the public health service, 100,000 in the building industry or 92,000 in public transport. Other researchers arrived at slightly different figures but they all agree that the armament industries yield the lowest rate of new jobs per sum invested; that is why it is an illusion to believe that the arms industry creates jobs. The real alternative is jobs *or* arms.

Research and development also play an important role. A report published by the OECD points out that most member states of NATO use almost 50 per cent of their gross public expenditure on research and development for military purposes. This percentage is considerably higher in the United States, as de Grasse and Gold showed in an article published in the *New York Times* in December 1981. At present, one-third of all American scientists and development engineers are working on armaments.

In view of these selective financial boosts for military research and development, we cannot support the hypothesis that the development of new weapon systems automatically outstrips negotiations on arms control and disarmament. There is a close interrelation between the difficulties encountered in these negotiations and the financial boosts given to military research and development, because both have the same source, the government's policy of military confrontation. It is no longer true that the results of military research merely reflect general developments in technology. It has become much more sophisticated. In fact, high subsidies for military research and development mean that comparable civilian branches have been left far behind. Today's armament producers make use of tomorrow's technological advances in forms so highly sophisticated that they can hardly be expected to be useful for other than military purposes.

We can consider only a few aspects of the problem here. One of them is the question of whether it is economically feasible to exhaust the Soviet Union by means of an arms race. In its disclosures about the Pentagon's guideline document, the *New York Times* described Defense Secretary Weinberger as ardently supporting a reduction in the Soviet Union's access to American and other non-Communist countries' technology. The Pentagon plan clearly reflects this approach. It also expresses the desire to implement a technology strategy aimed at undermining the economic power of the Soviet Union. According to the *New York Times*, this strategy requires massive investments in arms systems which will render existing Russian arsenals useless. This, in turn, will put the Russians to great expense and make it difficult for them to cope with their other vital problems.[24] To think, however, that this would exhaust Russia is yet another example of wishful thinking, for the following reasons:

firstly, the Soviet Union possesses material and technological resources and potential to permit a very efficient production of arms of all types, quite independently of the West;

secondly, the qualitative and quantitative capabilities of the Soviet Union and several other East European states in the fields of research, technology and science is often underestimated but they are perfectly adequate to achieve effective results in arms technology;

thirdly, the centralized system of management and decision making in the Warsaw Pact countries allows concentrated and efficient use to be made of all available means, if priority should be given to any particular objective.

It has not been possible to hinder the development of technology in the Soviet Union in the past and there is no fresh evidence to suggest that it would succeed today or in the future. But the repercussions on the West and the self-inflicted losses resulting from this strategy may turn out to be more dangerous. On 20 December 1982, *Newsweek* stated that 'more defence expenditure does not guarantee more national security'. That is true. A huge expenditure on armaments is made at the cost of social expenditure and the entire economy, not only of the USA but also of the West European countries, thanks to America's policy of confrontation. In a report of 29 November 1982, headed

'Guns vs. Butter', the magazine *Business Week* contrasted the increased expenditure on armaments with the cuts in social expenditure. On closer consideration, the Soviet Union need not even use its weapons since Weinberger and similarly-minded people are themselves seeing to it that large sections of the population will lose their jobs and homes; and whole branches of industry will be crippled; that governments will become incapacitated and that countries will be faced with economic ruin.

Imagine what could be achieved by a sensible use of the money spent annually for military purposes in NATO countries. In 1982, in Western Europe, the average expenditure per head of population, including infants and old people, was the equivalent of US$340 while in the United States it was $706 *per capita*. It is time to reverse this process. A freeze in military expenditure is synonymous with a freeze in armaments and an increase in social expenditure world-wide. Let us start there.

President Nixon has suggested diverting the confrontation with the Soviet Union from the military to the economic and political arena. He has diagnosed correctly the dangers inherent in a military confrontation but we should not allow the idea of confrontation to dominate in any field. The major problems of our times — environmental issues, international economic and financial relations and the sensible use of natural resources — can be solved only by cooperation, not confrontation. The structure of our society and the complexity of present-day production processes are too susceptible to the disruptions which aggressive behaviour promotes. International cooperation could draw the Soviet Union into a stable network of mutual interests. This would be a surer guarantee against war than military measures could ever be.

Towards a Military Policy
Serving Peace

Alternative defence concepts

The national armaments programmes of our allies, and the decisions made by NATO's leading committees, are still governed by the requirements of the strategy of flexible response, as we have already shown. Hence the importance of nuclear armament continues to grow within the overall range of military requirements.

The probability of any local conflict escalating into a nuclear war of total destruction is becoming greater. NATO's switch to nuclear policy and armament has always been controversial. Since the 1950s, when Colonel von Bonin put forward the concept of an army that relied on strong anti-tank and air defence forces to guarantee national security, the Federal Republic of Germany has been blue-printing defence concepts which are not based on nuclear armament. But so far successive governments of the Federal Republic and the senior staff of the Bundeswehr have opted for nuclear armament and have thus turned the Federal Republic into the country with the greatest density of nuclear arms — right on the border with the Warsaw Pact nations where a cautious political approach, especially in military matters, is imperative. But this would be incompatible with the 'victory in a nuclear war' thinking of leading advisers to the US president. This basic assumption, combined with the nuclear build-up, imposes a warfare orientated approach on all NATO military considerations which assume that any kind of conflict must end in the unconditional surrender of the adversary.

In his book *Vom Kriege* (*About War*), Karl von Clausewitz taught us that when planning for war, one must first consider the objective to be

[105]

achieved and then calculate the likely outcome.[1] During the Cuban crisis of 1962, President Kennedy provided an example both of a level-headed political assessment of the chances of victory in war, and of abstaining from senseless military operations with unimaginable results. After the danger of a nuclear world-wide war had been averted by constant dialogue with the then Soviet Prime Minister, Khruschev, Kennedy reasoned that the next urgent issue which had to be addressed was that of disarmament. With the danger past, priority should be given to the problem of non-proliferation of nuclear weapons on the earth and in outer space.[2] Washington unfortunately has chosen to ignore this assessment.

Nevertheless, for more than a decade NATO thought has been concerned with deliberating and debating the question of what could be achieved by war. This debate was fuelled in 1977 by reports from the USA that President Carter's Directive PRM10 planned to reduce tension on the borders with the Warsaw Pact countries by establishing that any Soviet attack should not be countered before it reached the Weser-Lech line. This proposed strategy, while raising the nuclear threshold, aroused considerable opposition from the West Germans because it would leave the eastern part of their territory undefended.

On 10 October 1977, Congressman Les Aspin explained this attitude in an interview with the magazine *Der Spiegel*: 'The Europeans have repeatedly expressed their wish for the use of tactical nuclear weapons at the earliest possible moment'. With a Conservative ascendancy in the USA, UK and the Federal Republic of Germany, a consensus was reached on both the strategy and deployment decisions of 1979. This stimulated the activities of the European peace movement and reactivated the public debate on strategy, based on the realization that traditional strategic thinking no longer takes account of the full destructive power of modern weapons. This is true of nuclear, conventional and other non-nuclear weapon systems. The change in conventional weapons includes an increase in accuracy, giving a significantly greater target-hitting effect. The efficiency of these new conventional weapons has been increased to such an extent that the gap between conventional and nuclear weapons is closing. The use of these weapons challenges all standards of conventional warfare to date and creates qualitatively new possibilities for defence and attack. Thus increased confrontation in the conventional range is also extremely dangerous.

Whatever the reason, most NATO military leaders support the

official strategic doctrines of the NATO member states. An allegedly indispensable and dominant component of these is the triad of nuclear systems (theatre, intermediate-range and strategic). However, concern about the feasibility of defence in NATO countries, based on the nuclear factor, is increasingly leading to the consideration of alternative concepts. The advocates of this thinking take into account the fact that security in the nuclear age can be achieved only if the policy intended for the prevention of war takes into consideration both one's own security interests and those of the potential opponent. That is why the models presently being devised for strengthening conventional defence are intended to create a credible defence strategy without the accompanying danger of self-extinction, while still representing an unacceptable risk to any would-be attacker. Such models have been developed by Steven L. Canby, Guy Brossolet, Horst Afheldt, Jochen Loeser, Alfred Mechtersheimer and others.*

Alternative concepts are based on conventional rather than nuclear forces, unlike the Rogers Plan which is supported by the Bundeswehr command and only provides for an increase in conventional forces in order to make it possible to combine nuclear and conventional forces more efficiently within the scope of the strategy of flexible response. We do not intend to differentiate between various models of 'area defence' and 'area-covering defence', but to assess the extent to which the models would still guarantee national defence requirements in the face of considerably reduced reliance on nuclear weapons, by either:

(a) providing a conventional defence which will increase the nuclear threshold but which would still be a strategic nuclear deterrence, or

(b) allowing for a conventional defence in Europe without any recourse to nuclear weapons.

According to these alternative concepts, current NATO strategy is not suited to the defence of the Alliance. The offensive forward defence plan which provides for an early transition to the use of nuclear weapons not only challenges and threatens the Warsaw Pact but — even more decisively — would lead to the complete destruction of the Federal Republic of Germany, Denmark and the Benelux countries. Any defence would be rendered useless. But both the model

---

*In the United Kingdom, the group Just Defence is currently developing the concept of non-provocative defence as a practical methodology and plans to present evidence of its viability to the British House of Commons Defence Committee in December 1984.

structures described above envisage a planning policy which abandons the principle of large-scale mobile warfare involving the employment of nuclear weapons. However, under model (a), the USA would still possess nuclear weapons at a supranational level as a preventive against the use of nuclear weapons by the Soviet Union. Instead of tank and armoured infantry units for offensive operations, a system of area-covering defence would be created. According to Loeser's ideas, it would be divided into three strategic sectors and could intercept and destroy an enemy attack by using infantry units heavily equipped with anti-tank systems.

There is, however, another group which sees no chance of survival for Western Europe in either a nuclear or a conventional war. For them political rather than military means for settling conflicts must be given priority and any security or military policies, especially in the armament field, which might impair confidence in international relations or challenge the security of the other side must be avoided. The defence policy of the NATO states should renounce the planning of all offensive operations, and dismantle the military structures and means of combat which exist for this purpose. National defence should be directed towards effectively securing the borders and be combined with a highly effective anti-tank and air defence. Unlike the former option, this one would reduce not only nuclear capabilities, but also military expenditures as a whole, thereby releasing finance for political and social development programmes. General Gert Bastian has proposed the following model for the Federal Republic of Germany:

Were, at some time in the future, the armed forces of West Germany not to participate in NATO's nuclear deterrence policy (or even go to war in the event of its failure), but instead have the task of securing its national borders against attack and making any aggressor pay highly for his aggression, then there is no need for them to be equipped as strongly and as expensively as the Bundeswehr is at present. In addition to having a clearer mission which can be explained to everybody and which no longer demands that in the event of war soldiers take part in the nuclear destruction of their homeland, there is another advantage: the possibility of significantly reducing expenditure for national defence. The considerable savings thus made in the defence budget will not only benefit domestic policy, but will also be significant in terms of foreign policy as a contribution by our country to the reduction of the arms race.

[108]

The most appropriate form of military defence for a non-aligned and neutral Federal Republic would be a combination of relatively small-scale active armed forces with a large-scale reinforcement army organized along the lines of a militia. This sort of defence has been adopted in different forms by non-aligned European countries and has achieved an impressive degree of efficiency in some cases. What matters most is not so much a reduction in the strength of the armed forces as expressing more clearly that all efforts undertaken are purely for self defence. This could be done by cancelling the offensive and furthermore particularly expensive components of the armed forces in favour of a home defence system based on modern defensive weapons.

The main body of the active forces should consist of army units, the majority of which could be subdivided into small combat units. Equipped with sophisticated surveillance and defence systems, these units would be designed to control and defend areas near the border. However, it should not be thought that this form of area defence in any way represents a kind of guerrilla warfare to be imposed upon the population. Such an idea would be wholly unacceptable. Units with tanks and armoured personnel carriers should be kept only for the support of key points. This means a drastic reduction in the number of these weapon systems presently maintained by the Bundeswehr. Modern air defence systems, ground support aircraft and anti-tank helicopters should be earmarked for the defence of national airspace and support of the ground troops, while all other offensive air fighting capabilities should be discarded.

The tasks of the navy would be restricted to direct coastal defence. Naval armament would therefore finally be reduced to small-scale combat vessels of various types, as well as to ground and air launched anti-ship missiles.

Besides the active armed forces, the milita-like reserve units should be an essential element in the national defence.[3]

Apart from the advantages and disadvantages of these alternative models, it is important to recognize that they are all based on the fact that not only is it possible to give up the nuclear defence component in Central Europe without loss of security, but that is it absolutely imperative for our survival that we do so. These models also justify calling a halt to the arms race. The existence of effective conventional weapons such as anti-tank and air defence systems guarantees an intolerably high rate of casualties for any aggressor without resorting to nuclear theatre weapons. Not only would defence requirements be

[109]

more cost effective, it would also recognize the true object of defence — to maintain national social and economic structures.

These alternative defence concepts could be given a firm basis if a de-nuclearization of the battlefield could be agreed upon through international negotiations between the two Alliances in Europe. A first step in this direction would be the adoption of the Palme proposal of 1983. This advocates creating a zone free of nuclear battlefield weapons across Central Europe. Unfortunately, this initiative was rejected by NATO, especially by the Federal Republic of Germany whose territory would mainly be affected. The only possible way to avert the danger of a nuclear conflict in Central Europe is to disengage nuclear capabilities and subsequently to reduce them. Mutual and parallel disengagement of nuclear battlefield weapons would provide a promising start and a real chance for a military strategy that guarantees our freedom.

Alternative defence concepts of this sort are credible not only as a military deterrence. Their value also consists — perhaps primarily — in reducing perceptions of threat and creating the material basis for the building of political and military confidence as well as supporting confidence building measures (CBM) in a narrower sense.

Confidence Building Measures (CBM)

Since the 1970s, consideration has been given to the kind of military intitiatives and measures that could be instituted to strengthen the political negotiations which have been in progress for more than a decade. Although the will was there, it was evident that, if the mutual distrust which has built up over the years is to be removed, additional step-by-step efforts are required to reduce that distrust.

Questions are constantly being asked that reflect our fundamental fear of aggression. 'Is the other side speaking the truth?' 'Will they respect agreements?' 'How will responsible military leaders react in a crisis?' 'Will any perceived weakness on the part of the other side be used as an excuse for a surprise attack?' In the years of détente, both East and West began to take their fears of each other as seriously as the negotiations themselves. It became obvious that some action must be taken if the defensive intentions of each side were to be clarified. These considerations were defined as Confidence Building Measures (CBM).

In the military context, the best known CBMs were incorporated into the Final Act (Agreement) of the 1975 Helsinki Conference on Security and Cooperation in Europe (CSCE). It was recommended that military manoeuvres carried out by one side should be notified in advance to the other and that, on a voluntary basis, observers from the other side should be invited to attend; the intention being to remove any fears that the manoeuvres would be used to mount a surprise attack. Situations where a country prepares for military aggression without the knowledge of other countries were to be forestalled. The resolving of problems of arms and troop verification, as part of the arms limitation process, was seen as being an all-important confidence building measure.

Since 1975, the experience in all respects has been positive. A new level of communication between East and West, stretching beyond the various negotiating levels, has been reached. The presence of foreign observers at manoeuvres makes it possible for each side to gain a more precise appreciation of the other's military thinking and the efficiency of its armed forces. It has resulted in more realistic assessments being made of the military situation. It has shown that confidence can be created only if the military and the politicians on each side come to know their counterparts and thereby gauge their likely reaction in crisis. The view taken by East and West of these arrangements and of the form other CBMs should take are very similar. They include:

— the notification of manoeuvres involving more than 25,000 men;
— an extension of the period notified for manoeuvres;
— the fixing of ceilings for the numbers taking part in manoeuvres;
— prohibition of multilateral manoeuvres near the borders of non-participating countries;
— compulsory notification of navy and air force manoeuvres.

During the SALT II negotiations, important agreements were reached which served confidence building, especially in the field of verification. These included:

— the rules for counting MIRVs;
— the obligation to notify certain kinds of tests;
— the clauses against the abuse of national technical means of verification.

No doubt these precedents will be indispensable to future negotiations. In addition, SALT II removed many obstacles by defining hitherto controversial positions and terms, so that they may now be used in the international strategy debate. Current and future negotiators will be spared the effort of defining terms; in this respect,

[111]

national and independent research centres have made an active contribution to confidence building. The general atmosphere of negotiations has been substantially improved by conferences of experts which thematically supported negotiations on all levels. A comprehensive list of military CBMs is now under discussion internationally. Various disarmament negotiations are dealing with the notification of manoeuvres and military movements and the exchange of observers as well as the disclosure of information on the strength and deployment of military manpower and the level of military expenditure. In addition, verification measures for disarmament agreements and the creation of mechanisms for consultation, especially for overcoming disagreements and for use during periods of crisis are also being discussed. Military missions and an exchange of delegations could be used to improve both contacts and mutual understanding, while a significant increase in stability could result from an extension of this confidence building process. The value of establishing contact at many levels is at last being realised. No real international interaction can occur without there being confidence and so, in its Final Act, the Madrid Conference on Security and Cooperation in Europe supported the proposal that CBMs should form the basis of the follow-up conference which opened in Stockholm in January 1984.

CBMs are guidelines for encouraging states voluntarily to renounce destabilizing activities which aggravate confrontation through military threats and aggressive propaganda. They are an integral part of the peace process in that real security can only be assured if there is cooperation between the parties to a dispute. CBMs have the purpose of defusing the fear and distrust created by the lack of information that countries have of each other's military activities. They are also able to contribute to the reaching of agreement between parties, even though they may be unable to rewrite the treaties on disarmament. Where confrontation exists, however, fear and distrust remain and confidence atrophies.

It is easy to understand why these CBMs — whether implemented or still under discussion — do not directly affect the extent of military power. So far, their security building effects have been relatively limited and designed for the short term. This is undoubtedly a result of their history. But we believe that CBMs could be extended beyond the military field. They could also become more binding and, if they were successful in achieving concrete results in disarmament negotiations, could directly influence conventional and nuclear weapon development.

On the one hand, the significance of CBMs is being increasingly recognized and awareness of their possibilities and limitations has grown to such an extent that, for the first time, an international conference is to be devoted solely to this problem. On the other hand, no new military CBMs have been agreed between East and West since 1975. With the renunciation of détente by the American government, the impetus for a strengthening of CBMs was unfortunately lost. Doubts about arms control and disarmament meant that CBMs were regarded as a kind of alternative strategy, or alibi. Vociferous support for CBMs could conceal an unchecked arms build up. The follow-up consideration of CBMs agreed upon in Helsinki has so far shown negative results, following a change of American policy.

Despite a formal adherence to guidelines for the notification of manoeuvres and the invitation of observers, NATO, in the late 1970s, substantially extended its manoeuvre activities and moved them closer to the borders with the Warsaw Pact. The number of troops involved increased as did the complexity of the exercises and the length of time units spent in the manoeuvres area.

There have also been attemtps to use the presence of observers for demonstrations of strength or for spying. This is a misuse of CBMs and damages their credibility. Nor is it accepted that the notification of or participation in manoeuvres can be conditional upon agreement relating to other unrelated issues such as human rights. Such actions would destroy rather than increase confidence, which can only result from actions and statements which express recognition of the other side's equality and respect for its security interests.

It is questionable whether CBMs of a purely military nature have a validity. The dialogue between the USA and USSR needs to be restored if the desire to end the confrontation is to be rekindled and if the preconditions are to be created whereby military CBMs could once again become effective. What the super-powers signal to one another is important. Their actions should encourage confidence building; unfortunately they do not. The US zero option proposal was an illusion. Their announcement of bigger and better armament programmes in the 1980s, the propagation of dangerous war strategies and the violent rhetoric of certain US statesmen have seriously prejudiced the chances of CBMs succeeding.

By contrast, the more recent proposals by the USSR suggest

establishing nuclear weapon-free zones, renouncing the use of force, unilateral arms reductions — even if these are dubious in some respects — and a readiness to agree on compromises regarding the problem of INF. These proposals are moving in the right direction. We value highly proposals emanating from third parties such as the United Nations, neutral and non-aligned countries and independent bodies such as the Palme commission. Scientific institutions have also put forward important proposals. The USA and USSR cannot ignore these ideas and proposals for ever, despite the difficulties of overcoming distrust. This at least is our hope, for it is high time to effect a positive response to new ideas. We recall the consequences of the delay in negotiations and the non-ratification of the SALT II treaty, when the gap widened between arms development and the results of negotiations. The speed of the arms build-up, especially in the fields of nuclear and missiles technology, is now so great that even the relative stability achieved on the strategic level could be endangered in future. Confidence building in the field of nuclear armament is rarely mentioned, though it would be of particular importance. Any measures which could destabilize the situation further should be rejected. Of the proposals put forward by retired General von Baudissin, formerly of the Hamburg Institute, and by the Palme commission, we think that the following are especially valuable and realistic:

— the renunciation of the development of nuclear first-strike weapons which would have a particularly destabilizing impact;
— maintenance of the 1972 ABM treaty;
— non-deployment of miniaturized nuclear and neutron weapons which obscure the difference between nuclear and conventional weapons;
— disclosure of information about the proportion of national budgets devoted to nuclear forces and research and development in this field;
— notification of submarine patrols passing a certain border in peacetime;
— notification of the movements of nuclear weapons and mobile delivery systems for training purposes;
— extension of the early warning period by separately stockpiling rockets, launching mechanisms and warheads;
— establishment of an international agency for reconnaissance satellites to improve verification measures;

- agreements on a moratorium in research, development and deployment;
- improvement in crisis management including stopping of all nuclear manoeuvres during periods of tension.[4]

In Europe, two kinds of CBM are of special importance: those prohibiting the use of military power to exert political pressure and those which decrease the danger of a surprise attack. The Swedish proposal to create a nuclear weapon-free zone in Central Europe and, more generally, regional security programmes for the creation of 'peace zones' (Balkan Peninsula, Mediterranean Sea, Scandinavia) are both relevant in this context. Not surprisingly, there are objections and reservations about many aspects of these proposals in both East and West, but there is also a large degree of common interest. *All* proposals are worth discussing. They can influence the climate of negotiations in a positive way, but they will only be effective and lasting if they are followed by progress in treaties between the military alliances. Only the will to achieve results is required and that brings us to our final comment on the conduct of negotiations, with special reference to the Madrid CSCE conference.

In view of the deadlock which exists at negotiating levels, a realistic approach becomes almost a confidence building measure in itself. Naturally, both sides have the right and the duty to define their own ideas and aims as precisely as possible. But they must not be submitted as ultimatums which exclude the possibility of compromise. It is also impossible to present all the topics of the CSCE process in a package of negotiating conditions. We regard this sort of use of a uniform CSCE process as a pretext for obstructing progress. Western negotiators should remember the principle which produced undoubted successes in the treaty policy of the early 1970s.

Differences in areas where agreement could not be reached were not allowed to obstruct those areas where progress could be made. A renunciation of preconditions is promising and constructive, as is a willingness to discuss all other ideas appropriate to the issue under negotiation. In the long run, we cannot afford to dismiss the other side's proposals out of hand as being 'attempts at intimidation' or 'threats'. Nor can we treat them with disdain. We must carefully study them and respond contructively. There are already enough proposals on the table to make a European disarmament conference a matter of some urgency.

Disarmament — the Need
of the Moment

Greater security with fewer weapons — is it an illusion?

A defence policy which aims at maintaining state sovereignty and at safeguarding the material as well as the biological substance of a country would — in connection with alternative strategies and confidence building measures — doubtless encourage and facilitate arms control and disarmament as a step towards alternative strategies and confidence building. A world without weapons would be a world without the means of exercizing military power. We all know that the existing arsenals are sufficient to destroy the civilization which we are ostensibly preserving and defending. Deeply rooted in stereotyped patterns of thought established by centuries of experience, we truly believe that more weapons mean more security. Resignedly, many honest and critical people are realizing that, in spite of verbal declarations in favour of peace and disarmament, the level of military confrontation has risen steadily, not only between the East and the West, but also in many other areas of the world. The number and quality of weapons stockpiled — and ready to be used — has increased continuously. Both national and international security have become more fragile, rather than stronger. It is obvious that security cannot be achieved by a quantitative and qualitative increase in armaments, but why not?

One major factor, repeatedly demonstrated in the course of history, is that there can be no permanent monopoly of armaments, either quantatively or qualitatively. Gunpowder, the machine-gun, tanks and nuclear weapons provided only a limited and temporary advantage for those who used them first; an advantage, moreover, that

[116]

had to be paid for dearly when others caught up. Revolutions in military technology do not have victors. Humanity has always been the loser, as the increasing numbers of people killed in wars have shown.

The second main reason is that modern nuclear weapons of mass destruction make an effective defence virtually impossible. The only protection against such a weapon is to prevent its use, but it does not look as if this will be militarily possible in the foreseeable future. The danger and destructive potential of modern nuclear systems can neither be eliminated by more armament nor adequately limited by protective measures.

A third important reason is the fact that modern weapons are so costly — in the broadest sense of the word — that armament becomes politically and economically destabilizing. Therefore it endangers rather than guarantees security.

If democratic and social achievements are sacrificed to the Moloch of armament and militarization, in an atmosphere of political confrontation, one destroys that which is worth defending. At the same time, by concentrating on the East–West conflict we are stopping ourselves from constructively approaching the North–South conflict, which is just as important for the future of mankind. We are prevented from tackling these problems for idealistic and political reasons but also, and possibly mainly, because important financial and material resources are tied up in the totally unproductive arms race.

Despite these understandable reasons, the production of armaments has continued at a greater pace than ever before. Are we thus bound to conclude that a cessation, limitation or reduction of armament is only an illusion and that a world without weapons and violence is no more than an Utopian vision? Were we to agree with this view, it would be as good as denying that mankind is capable of acting rationally and of surviving. The whole of history, however, has proved that mankind is able to learn — even if this is more clearly demonstrated in the scientific and technical field than in the socio-political world.

Nevertheless, arms limitation and disarmament are necessary if we do not want one day to fall victim — either deliberately or by accident — to the destructive forces we ourselves have created and which we are continuing to stockpile. More and more people are coming to understand this. It is encouraging that they are and it is an important precondition for solving this problem. Equally important is that results and experiences exist to prove that the limitation and reduction of

[117]

military confrontation is feasible. Thus neither the necessity nor the feasibility of arms limitation and disarmament can be denied on principle. In this sense, it was not Utopian for the Final Document of the first UN Special Session on Disarmament in 1978 to advocate gradual disarmament, and to state: 'While the final objective of the efforts of all states should continue to be general and complete disarmament under effective international control, the immediate goal is that of the elimination of the danger of a nuclear war and the implementation of measures to halt and reverse the arms race and clear the path towards lasting peace'.[1]

In the past, political understanding and goodwill have shown that it is possible to find solutions which are not only acceptable to both sides, but also helpful. A limitation and reduction in the level of military confrontation therefore cannot be seen merely as a game which one side wins at the expense of the other. Neither should such agreements be regarded as a concession or a sacrifice. Both sides would gain the advantage of increased security — something which cannot be achieved by arms or military measures. A basic requirement, of course, is acceptance of the view that security has priority over war as the fundamental and essential security interest. The process of détente was given an important impetus in the light of this opinion. The US President John F. Kennedy, said in a speech at Washington University on 10 June 1963:

> What kind of peace do we seek? Not a Pax Americana enforced on the world by American weapons of war. I speak of peace because of the new face of war. Total war makes no sense in an age when great powers can maintain large and relatively invulnerable nuclear forces and refuse to surrender without resort to those forces. . . . I speak of peace as the sensible aim of sensible people. . . . Some people think that we do not need to talk about world peace, international law or international disarmament; that it is pointless as long as the leaders of the Soviet Union do not adopt an enlightened attitude. I assume that the Soviet leaders will. . . . But I also believe that we must examine our own attitudes, as individuals and as a nation, because our attitudes are as important as theirs. . . . If we cannot settle our differences, we can still contribute to making the world in its variety a safer place.[2]

The discrepancy between Kennedy's views and the schools of thought current in Washington today is unmistakable. But it does not prove that Kennedy's considerations are no longer valid. Instead, it indicates the historical regression reflected in Reagan's thinking and behaviour. The results achieved so far on the basis of Kennedy's philosophy indicate that his attitude was correct. One can, of course, argue that the results have not been comprehensive enough to stop the arms race. This is undoubtedly true. But it is unjustified to deny their importance or, even worse, simply to dismiss them as manoeuvres designed to appease the anti-arms policy lobby and as a strategy for misleading the public and preserving the superiority of the super powers. History does not allow such an interpretation.

Let us look, therefore, at a few examples which can teach us an historical lesson. We shall examine some of the results achieved by negotiation and détente which today have a particular relevance to the maintenance of peace and reduction of military confrontation. One example is the signing of the International Austrian Treaty on 15 May 1955. In cooperation with Austria, the governments of the USA, the Soviet Union, Great Britain and France agreed to withdraw their occupation forces from Austrian territory and to grant and guarantee it neutral status on the model of Switzerland. This international treaty bound Austria not to join any military pact, not to allow foreign military bases on its territory, to renounce the possession of nuclear, biological, chemical and other weapons of mass destruction and to accept limitations of its own military capability.

This treaty and its political consequences, which removed a potential trouble spot, were seen as a safeguard of peace and stability in Europe. It is a pity that an analagous solution is not possible for Germany because of its division into two parts. Instead, it has a foot in both Alliances. A comparison of Austria and the two German states shows that neutrality does not have the same negative implications for a security policy that membership of a military pact has. The example of Austria demonstrates that the renunciation of nuclear, biological and chemical weapons, the limitation of military capabilities and the exclusion of foreign military bases does not result in a loss of national sovereignty, security or ability for political action. With regard to the economic situation in Austria, it could be suggested that the renunciation of high military expenditure together with the economic opportunities flowing from its neutral status have enabled Austria to avoid most of the effects of the world-wide crisis. Apart from the benefit for Austria and its people, this example allows us to draw some fundamental conclusions:

[119]

firstly, a result was achieved through negotiations and compromise which would have been unthinkable if the threat of violence or military action had been employed;

secondly, as a result of negotiations, military forces were spread out more widely and military confrontation was relaxed, defusing potential trouble spots and conflict areas within the region, thus creating an advantageous situation for all the parties concerned;

thirdly, as far as stability is concerned, this solution has proved to be successful. Over almost thirty years, Austria has developed its own political and social order. It has become a highly-esteemed member of the United Nations' community of states;

fourthly, the Soviet Union is able and willing to keep treaties and to guarantee their fulfilment. The Soviet Union has never tried to blackmail Austria by political, economic or military intimidation, nor has it attempted to interfere in Austria's domestic or foreign policy decisions. Therefore, to confront the Soviet Union with the threat of force of arms seems senseless. The point is often made that it is NATO which has guaranteed Austria's freedom and has thus deterred the Soviet Union from taking action against Austria. But is this logic conclusive when reduced to military considerations? The Soviet attitude is most probably dictated by the Austrians' conviction that the Western system is preferable to 'existing socialism'. The assertion that the Soviet Union's foreign policy is dictated by an aggressive claim to power, that it is striving, by force, for a world-wide victory for Communism, simply contradicts the Communist tenet that it is not possible to 'export revolution'. Austria has shown how, in real terms, a country can direct its national policy to the promotion of peace and security and not to expansion. If more were to adopt this approach it would be possible to develop a truly constructive policy which could achieve more than any military confrontation can. It would substantiate the truth that military confrontation only gets in the way of political solutions.

Austria is not the only example of a political solution that results in a reduction of military confrontation. Finland too has shown that political reason and goodwill can achieve more than military intimidation and confrontation strategies. Free to make its own decisions on political and social matters, domestic and foreign policy, Finland undoubtedly has a more secure physical and political existence than those countries whose territory is bristling with launching sites for nuclear missiles and toxic gas depots, and whose

[120]

sovereignty is reduced through membership of a military alliance. Those who belittle the neutrality of Sweden, Switzerland and Austria and believe that the 'Finlandisation' of Western Europe would be intolerable are probably reacting to their own awareness of the inadequacies of their national policies on security.

The Cuban crisis — or Cuban missile crisis, as it has gone down in history — provided an important experience of crisis management and of how a constructive solution to a crisis may be found in the nuclear age. At that time, the USA deployed nuclear medium-range missiles in Western Europe which were directed against the USSR. As the Soviet Union was not able to counter with an equivalent, it decided to deploy Soviet intermediate-range missiles on Cuba — the USA's doorstep. It is probable that the move was also intended as a deterrent to the continuous attacks made on Cuba by the CIA, which were carried out with the approval of the US Administration. Aerial photography led to the discovery of the missiles on Cuba and the subsequent escalation of the crisis brought the world to the brink of a third world war. Thanks, however, to the level-headedness of Kennedy and his counterpart Khruschev, the crisis was defused and the conflict settled peacefully. The Soviet Union withdrew its missiles from Cuban territory. The USA guaranteed to stop its invasion attempts against Cuba and tacitly withdrew its medium-range missiles stationed in Western Europe (their function was taken over by nuclear submarines carrying missiles in the Mediterranean and North Atlantic). Several of the politicians who had been members of the crisis handling committee and responsible for the decision making stated in memoirs that Kennedy was not aiming to 'punish' the Soviet Union, but was looking for a constructive settlement of the conflict because he was aware of the irrelevance of America's nuclear superiority: the Soviet Union had sufficient nuclear weapons to inflict a degree of damage on the USA which was quite unacceptable and which far exceeded Cuba's value to the USA. This sensible attitude resulted in a compromise solution which decreased the regional level of military confrontation and made both super-powers aware of the necessity to limit the dangers which inevitably arise from a nuclear confrontation.

Thus the Cuban crisis became the starting point for numerous bilateral and multilateral treaties and agreements directed towards the limitation of risks resulting from the development of modern nuclear weapon systems. Ultimately, these treaties should apply to the weapon systems themselves.

[121]

The transition from Cold War to détente in East–West relations was further advanced by the signing in Washington on 1 December 1959 of the Antarctic Treaty, whereby the use of that region for military purposes was forbidden. The process of transition was not affected by either the building of the Berlin Wall or the Cuban crisis, and survived the Vietnam war. It was the result of such a realistic approach that it was possible to achieve some political progress during this period, not least the continuation of the SALT II talks. The areas of risk were identified and the extent to which either side could exert influence on the other was better understood. Against this background one initiative deserves particular mention. In 1969 Valerian Zorin (USSR) and John McCloy (USA) drew up an agreement which served as a basis for a whole series of bilateral disarmament talks between the two countries. The Zorin–McCloy Agreement was presented to the UN General Assembly on 20 September 1961. It embodied important principles, including the implementation and supervision of phased disarmament measures and the principles of equality and equal security, and serves as a sound basis for peace-building initiatives even today.

The American-Soviet agreement of 20 June 1963 created a direct communication link ('hot line' or 'red telephone') between the two Heads of State and reflected both sides' concern over the grave consequences which might result from errors, misinterpretations or failures in strategic weapon systems, or from the sudden escalation of 'brush fire wars'.

Two treaties followed: the Banning of Nuclear Weapon Tests in the Atmosphere, Outer Space and Underwater of 5 August 1963, and the Peaceful Use of Outer Space, 27 January 1967, whose positive effects defied rejection. Though the limiting of nuclear testing has not impeded the technological development of nuclear weapons, undoubtedly it has prevented our environment being exposed to an increase in the level of radioactivity. Though the treaty on the use of space for peaceful means has affected the development and testing of space weapons, one would wish that the controls were tighter. It is still possible that space will be used as a weapon deployment area; as the United States has already indicated this with their plans for stationing laser weapons and cosmic battle stations in space as an extension of their defence system.

On 25 June 1968 — in what came to be known as the 'signal from Reykjavik' — NATO submitted its proposals for mutual and balanced force reductions in Europe, which paved the way for the MBFR talks in Vienna.

The signing of the Non-Proliferation Treaty and its subsequent endorsement by the overwhelming majority of the member states of the United Nations was of the utmost importance. The treaty closely interrelates with those regional treaties and agreements which aim to ban the possession, storage, production and/or use of nuclear weapons, thus guaranteeing nuclear-free zones in the various regions. The Treaty of Tlatelolco, 14 February 1967, dealt with the prohibition of nuclear weapons in Latin America and serves the same purpose, as does UN resolution 2033(XX) for a nuclear-free zone in Africa. The fact that these treaties have failed to win universal acceptance obviously reduces their effectiveness, but it would be wholly wrong to conclude therefore that they have no value and are of no consequence. On the contrary, they have played an important part in the moral reassessments and commitments which a number of states have made regarding possession of nuclear weapons. The treaties have validated the conviction that we should dispense with nuclear weapons. It would be wrong to assess the impact of these treaties on what they have not achieved; rather they should be judged by the fact that they have succeeded in slowing down the proliferation of the nuclear arms race and in codifying in terms of international law some of the more important basic principles of détente. Thus it has been possible to exclude certain areas from the arms race, and to assert control in such a way that the comparable levels necessary for arms limitation and disarmament talks have been maintained.

By the same token, the Treaty on the Prohibition of the Deployment of Nuclear Weapons and Other Weapons of Mass Destruction on the Sea-Bed and the Ocean Floor and in the Subsoil Thereof, 11 February 1971, served the same purpose. It was followed by a series of treaties which were to be signed in the course of the negotiations on strategic arms limitation between the USA and the Soviet Union; included among them was the Treaty on the Limitation of Anti-Ballistic Missile Systems, 26 May 1972, and a temporary agreement between the USSR and the USA on measures in the field of limiting strategic offensive weapons, which contained a supplementary protocol and an agreement on the basis of their bilateral relations at that time. It stated that both countries would begin from the common understanding that in the nuclear age there is no alternative to peaceful co-existence as the basis of their relationship. Existing differences between the ideological and social systems of the US and the USSR should be no obstacle to the bilateral development of normal relations based on the principles of sovereignty, equality, mutual benefit and non-intervention in domestic affairs. Both sides would continue their efforts for arms limitation on a bilateral as well as a multilateral level; they would undertake particular efforts to limit strategic armament and they would try to conclude concrete agreements to realize their objectives whenever possible. The USSR and the USA considered it their final objective to solve the problems of general and comprehensive disarmament and to develop an effective system of international security in accordance with the aims and principles of the United Nations Organization.[3]

Subsequently, numerous treaties and agreements were signed which were of great importance in stabilizing the international situation and the relationship of the USA and the Soviet Union. They include:
— Agreement on Basic Principles of Negotiations on the Further Limitation of Strategic Offensive Weapons, 21 June 1973;
— Agreement on Co-operation in the Field of the Use of Nuclear Energy for Peaceful Purposes, 21 June 1973;
— Agreement on the Prevention of Nuclear War, 22 June 1973;
— annexe to the Treaty on the Limitation of Anti-Ballistic Missile Systems, 31 July 1974;
— Treaty on the Limitation of Underground Nuclear Weapon Tests, 3 July 1974;
— Joint Statement on the Limitation of Strategic Offensive Weapons, signed at Vladivostock on 24 November 1974.

In the light of Washington's current policies, it is imperative that we should remind ourselves of these treaties. The interrelation between limiting strategic arms and anti-ballistic missile systems must not be forgotten at a time when President Reagan is planning to station radiation weapons in space and to exchange mutual deterrence for unilateral deterrence and strategic superiority. It is also important to remember that these treaties acknowledged the fact that peaceful co-existence is the only basis for American-Soviet relations, and recognized the principles of sovereignty, equality and non-intervention in the domestic affairs of other states which are involved, including the commitment to limit arms. By departing from these principles, US policy has not been more successful; instead the international situation has deteriorated and the danger of nuclear war has increased.

Numerous agreements of the utmost importance for the development of security and cooperation between the European states have also been closely linked to bilateral American-Soviet treaties. Both processes — the bilateral American-Soviet negotiations and the bilateral and multilateral negotiations important for Europe — occurred simultaneously. It is possible therefore to assess the value of the relationship that exists between the two super-powers for the settlement of international problems on a world-wide scale. At the same time, it is evident that the development of American–Soviet relations did not take place separately from European concerns, let alone at their expense. In spite of Washington's present policy of confrontation and armament, the European states are not willing to allow the principles of the policy of détente and cooperation to be completely destroyed, clearly demonstrating the importance they attach to the policy which emanated over that period.

The effect of this policy can best be characterized by those treaties entered into by the Federal Republic of Germany and a number of East European states, including the Soviet Union, with the soubriquet 'Ostvertraege'. Other relevant multilateral agreements were:

— the agreement of 28 June 1973 to begin negotiations on the mutual reduction of forces and armaments in Central Europe and other connected measures. This agreement provided the foundation for the MBFR negotiations which began on 30 October 1973 in Vienna and are still continuing;

— The Final Act of the Helsinki Conference on Security and Cooperation in Europe, 1 August 1975, which embraced a series of agreements on confidence building measures and other issues relating to security and disarmament, including recognition of the European borders created as a result of the Second World War. (The Helsinki Conference on European Security and Cooperation has been followed by a second in Madrid (1982–83) and even more recently by the Disarmament and Confidence Building Conference in Stockholm in January 1984. *Ed.*)

The USA, followed to a certain extent by the governments of Western Europe, abandoned the policy of détente without having exhausted its potential. The second strategic arms limitation agreement — SALT II — was signed by both sides but it was not ratified by the USA. The policy of détente was denounced as favouring Soviet armament and expansionist aims. It was superseded by a political line which replaced a rational approach to foreign and

[125]

security policy with verbal demonstrations of strength and a sense of hopelessness about the arms race, in which there can only be losers.

In assessing the policy of détente, it has to be admitted that no rational alternative exists, but it would be wrong to jump to the conclusion that this will always be the case and criticize détente on those grounds. People who take this view lack resolve and are likely to end up on the wrong track. Even if the first attempts went too far for some, it must be realized that peace and international security today are suffering from too little détente, not too much.

If we seek solutions to all international problems, including military ones, while at the same time radically curtailing our political contacts and negotiating only in order to 'keep up appearances', we shall side-step the issues which constrain us in our present situation. Today, confrontation as a means of providing an answer to our problems has been shown to be ineffective, and more and more people are coming to realise this despite all the propaganda to the contrary. The enormous nuclear arsenals need to be reduced, not increased. The survival of our planet requires not blustering, but mutual restraint, political shrewdness and military caution. Current American policy seems to be moving further and further away from these indispensable premises, in spite of domestic resistance from responsible politicians and military leaders. The circles around President Reagan and his Defense Secretary Caspar Weinberger obstinately oppose the view that arms control and disarmament are immediately necessary in order to reduce the level of military confrontation. They lack the essential prerequisite for achieving this — political resolution. Arms control and disarmament are possible only if there is a visible determination to succeed. The necessity for comparing very different weapon systems, for taking into consideration complicated political factors, for addressing ourselves to the question of national and international control and to the prevention of the development of new stabilizing weapons which would undermine existing agreements on arms limitation or disarmament — all these make great demands on the goodwill of both sides. Every day, technical problems create difficulties which, if one side lacks the resolution to arrive at an effective result, can always be used as an excuse to break off negotiations. The determination to succeed must be combined with the acknow-ledgement of certain principles of negotiation. If these are not respected, all assurances lack credibility and, in the final analysis, are worthless. The most important of these principles are:

- an acknowledgement of the legitimate security interests of the other side, and of the equality of both negotiating partners;
- an awareness that security cannot be guaranteed by armament, but only destroyed by it, and that security cannot be achieved in opposition to the other side, but only in cooperation with it;
- the desire to restrict areas of conflict and to extend détente — not the desire to make conflicts worldwide and to restrict détente;
- the limitation of military power as an element of foreign policy, and the rejection of a policy which attempts to achieve security primarily by military means and therefore strives for military superiority.

Armament represents a heavy burden. Undoubtedly, the willingness of the Soviet Union to negotiate and compromise is more than mere talk; the opportunity must be used. It would be dangerous, however, to attempt to put it to the test by striving uncompromisingly for one-sided political and military advantages. Negotiations cannot and must not be regarded as a concession to the Soviet Union; they are equally in the interests of NATO. If it were possible to agree only on a freeze in armaments, NATO countries would save billions of dollars which could be used to safeguard jobs and for social welfare. Even more valuable would be the increase in security that this would bring about, since a freeze in armaments would indicate that the political elements of security policy had at last been adequately acknowledged. This would be the true, the decisive breakthrough. If one is not prepared to negotiate constructively, it is impossible to devise an effective security policy in the current world situation.

It is therefore a grave political mistake to dismiss all the proposals made by the Soviet Union as mere propaganda. It would, of course, be equally mistaken to expect proposals to take the form of 'gifts'. If one wants anything, it will always be necessary to give something in exchange. However, peace and security, at present extremely costly in terms of arms expenditure, should be worth political compromises. What is preventing us from taking the Soviet Union at its word, and testing its willingness to negotiate? At the meeting of the Warsaw Pact's Committee of Political Advisers in Prague on 4–5 January 1983, several interesting proposals were made which certainly deserve more than a grudging 'test':
- no further increase in armament and troop levels and a freeze on nuclear arsenals;
- agreements on calling a halt to the development and production of

[127]

new nuclear weapon systems, as well as on the production of fissionable material for the manufacture of various types of weapons;
- the conclusion of a treaty concerning a comprehensive and general ban on the testing of nuclear weapons (Comprehensive Test-Ban Treaty);
- the drawing-up of a convention on the prohibition and destruction of chemical weapons;
- a ban on the deployment of all weapons in outer space;
- a convention concerning a ban on radiological weapons;
- a decrease in the level of conventional armament and numbers of troops as well as a restriction on the arms trade;
- a limitation of military activities at sea and the removal of foreign military bases and the withdrawal of foreign troops from the territories of other countries;
- a freeze on armaments expenditure, followed by cutbacks in proportional and then absolute terms;
- agreements on the prevention of a new round of the arms race in Europe and — as the ideal solution — the creation of a Europe free of tactical and intermediate-range nuclear weapons.

The positive attitude displayed by the Eastern bloc towards the Swedish suggestion of a nuclear-free zone in Europe fits this context. As already mentioned, the German Democratic Republic has expressed its willingness to make its entire territory available for such a zone.

Genuine results depend on the positions from which negotiations start. Results will not be achieved unless negotiations are based on:
- an acknowledgement of the political and territorial status quo;
- a realistic assessment, not influenced by political motives, of the balance of military forces and its components;
- a willingness to regulate existing imbalances in certain types of nuclear weapons which, because of the capacity of each side to destroy the potential opponent several times over, are of no significance and can be ignored;
- an awareness that further armament only creates new dangers without pointing any way out of that danger, while disarmament is a course of action orientated towards the future.

The pressure to negotiate and to compromise is seemingly greater in Europe than it is in the USA. But the world cannot wait for America's leading politicians to realize that the dangers of the nuclear age will not stop at America's borders.

Only results count

It is commonly believed that while negotiations continue the shooting will not start. But negotiations ultimately succeed or fail and therefore have to be purposeful. We need to remember this and the consequences which could occur if negotiations are nothing more than a facade to calm public opinion and not to achieve meaningful results. In the present US Administration, President Reagan has appointed a number of senior officials who are on record as being opposed to détente with the Russians and to serious negotiations on arms control. Their political viewpoint alone is a clear indication that progress in the arms talks is unlikely.

Eugene Rostow, until recently the holder of they key appointment of Director of the Arms Control and Disarmament Agency, may have come to reject the pretence of negotiating under false colours and thus had to be replaced. He was co-founder of the conservative Committee on the Present Danger, set up in President Carter's time as an anti-Communist lobby. When the Republicans came to power, members of this Committee were given senior posts which related directly to the conduct of arms and security negotiations with the Soviet Union. In its time the Committee successfully opposed the ratification of the SALT II agreement, calling it 'a step towards war'. Kenneth Adelman, Rostow's dangerously inexperienced successor, has left no doubt in people's minds as to his personal credo regarding the USSR.

Another key figure in this hierarchy is the retired Lieutenant-General, Edward Rowny, head of the USA's START negotiating delegation which set out with the intention of reducing strategic arms systems — especially those of the Soviet Union. In 1979 he resigned from America's SALT II negotiating delegation in protest at what he felt was the Carter Administration's undue readiness to compromise with the Soviet Union. Early in 1983 Rowny, reappointed by President Reagan, attracted public attention by questioning the political and professional competence of almost every member of the START delegation on the grounds that they favoured a more conciliatory approach in the talks. He recommended their dismissal to Adelman.

Paul Nitze, longstanding head of the INF negotiating delegation, became weary of the SALT negotiations and retired in 1972. In the autumn of 1977, *International Security* published a number of articles by Nitze on the stages of nuclear war. He is a specialist on concepts of regional limited nuclear warfare — particularly in the European context.

Reagan's policy in choosing his team shows that arms control is an integral part of his policy of military supremacy and confrontation towards the Soviet Union. It finds its expression in the anti-Soviet, anti-détente political appointees who in one way or another participate in arms limitations and disarmament talks; such people as William Casey, CIA chief, Jeane Kirkpatrick, UN Ambassador, and Max M. Kampelman, head of the US delegation to the Madrid Conference. The activities of these politicians do not necessarily invalidate the chances for agreements on disarmament, indeed there is growing opposition to their negative approach to negotiations and for misleading the public. Illusions of waging 'Star Wars' on earth and deploying new radiation weapons which destabilize the parity already existing in the military strategic field must be replaced by an early move towards stabilization and a reversal of the arms race.

The first and most urgent requirement is for an immediate halt to and freeze of nuclear armaments. We have already pointed out that there are more than enough nuclear weapons and that their proliferation will only create greater insecurity and danger. There is a basic logic in the view that before the nuclear arms race can be reversed, it has to be frozen. An equally important step is the banning of the development, testing and deployment of new systems of nuclear and other weapons of mass destruction. Previous treaties such as that on the limitation of ABM systems have pointed the way towards blocking certain developments in military technology. Building on these experiences, a complete halt is achievable in most of the destabilized and threatening fields of arms developments.

At present, the gravest danger arises from the increasing proliferation and development of new types of nuclear weapons and their corresponding carrier and delivery systems, but the difficulties are not confined to limiting or reducing strategic and medium-range nuclear systems and any new types of weapons of mass destruction make the danger all that greater. Even though some form of control may be imposed over existing weapons, there are opportunities for the development of new weapons which are even more dangerous than those we already have and whose existence could preempt a higher level of confrontation than before. Radical cuts in military research and development budgets, the banning of the developing and testing of new weapons and the introduction of effective controls are some of the ways by which the danger can be averted. One problem is more urgent than others; the problem of guaranteeing an effective control over the acquisition of a unilateral destabilizing capability by one side, while advances continue in science and technology and the development of smaller but more effective weapons. Each day it becomes increasingly important that we halt particularly dangerous developments by concluding appropriate agreements. These developments include:

— the further minaturization of nuclear weapons and their carrier and delivery systems;
— the bulk production and use of nuclear weapons such as Cruise missiles and the blurring of differences between conventional and nuclear systems;
— the deployment of weapon systems requiring 'launch on warning', which eliminate time as a safety factor but use it to gain superiority;
— the use of stealth techniques, that is, design methods which impede identification and detection of weapon systems;
— the deployment of nuclear weapons of mass destruction close to national borders. In the case of conflict, this would allow not a flexible response but nuclear escalation;
— the extension of anti-missile systems limited by the ABM treaty which is now in danger of being circumvented;
— any militarization of outer space.

Modern military technology is capable of countering action by the peace movement simply because of the speed at which it is able to produce new weapons of mass destruction. Neutron bombs, inter-mediate-range weapons, new chemical warfare agents, the militarization of outer space and the development of radiation weapons have advanced so fast that it is no longer possible to react to each of these developments. The pace of development and introduction of new weapon systems will perhaps increase even more if the process of armament cannot be halted altogether.

Renunciation by *all* parties of the first use of nuclear weapons would make for a major increase in confidence. The Soviet Union has already announced in a far from noncommittal declaration its readiness to renounce a first strike. Moreover, it calls for a commitment to a defence philosophy for which nuclear superiority is irrelevant, and which opposes the theory that it is possible to wage and win a nuclear

[131]

war. It puts nuclear weapons into the category of political weapons, thereby carrying the risk of retaliatory attack and the danger of self-destruction to the user. Renunciation of first use means a military strategy orientated to defence and a realistic assessment of the risks of nuclear war; it affects not only the basic orientation of military strategy, but also important problems such as the non-proliferation of nuclear weapons and the security interests of countries without nuclear weapons. It is well-known that a number of prominent American politicians have taken a realistic attitude towards these problems and support a renunciation of first use of nuclear weapons while at the same time rejecting the Reagan Administrations's policy of escalating a nuclear confrontation.

Further important matters for consideration are the creation of a nuclear-free zone and, above all, the withdrawal of nuclear weapons from the border between the two most powerful blocs of Central Europe. Sweden's proposal had a mixed reception. While the Warsaw Pact countries welcomed it and expressed interest, NATO's attitude, based on the conviction that a nuclear defence is possible, was negative.

Finally, a moratorium on the testing, production and deployment of new nuclear weapons would be a promising way of halting the nuclear arms race and initiating successful and effective negotiations on arms limitation and disarmament, besides giving a fillip to negotiations for disarmament. Jerome Wiesner, scientific adviser to Presidents Kennedy and Johnson, wrote in the *New York Times* that:

> President Reagan should declare an open-ended unilateral moratorium of new nuclear weapons and delivery systems. He should invite the Soviet Union to respond with a parallel declaration of purpose.... The call is for action, not negotiation.... How long would it take to negotiate a 'balanced' freeze? A moratorium undertaken independently by the nuclear states is a safe way out of this dilemma. Ending the arms race with a moratorium means dispensing with the need to match weapon for weapon and to seek a numerical balance.... A moratorium is a way of arresting the arms race. What we ultimately do and how far we finally go beyond this easy initial stage depends upon how each side responds. The unilaterally agreed moratorium should be just a first step in global psychotherapy.[4]

However, it would seem from past record that Moscow would be more prepared than Washington to translate a responsible proposal such as this into action. A moratorium could improve substantially the climate of negotiation, provided its purpose is to make a positive contribution to political and military confidence building. But it will not solve the fundamental problems of the growth of military confrontation. This requires constructive dialogue at all negotiating levels. We must be aware that long-term armament programmes exist while analogous plans for disarmament are lacking. Military peacekeeping measures are pursued far more systematically and professionally than a disarmament policy which involves political understanding. America's Arms Control and Disarmament Agency has lost much of its credibility and impact as a result of its staffing inadequacies; its budget is less than that of the United States military bands! This reflects the low degree of importance that the United States currently attaches to its arms limitation and disarmament policy.

Other NATO countries lack any institutions for dealing with disarmament policy. Thus there is no administrative system to balance against the demands and interests of an established military hierarchy and it is no wonder that the positions adopted by individual NATO countries during arms and disarmament negotiations often derive from disagreements between their different government ministries and are easily reversed by the more comprehensive plans which the foremost states submit.

It is not merely a matter of establishing a government agency responsible for arms control and disarmament. The decisive factor is its political authority and the extent to which this is recognized in government policy. Characteristically, the USA established such an agency at a time when the government found it necessary to negotiate strategic arms limitation with the Soviet Union due to new political and military conditions created by the development of weapons of nuclear mass destruction. Outstanding individuals in US political life put their stamp on this agency's activities; people like Gerard Smith and Paul Warnke enjoy a world-wide reputation. But as the idea of strategic arms limitations was given up and replaced by a policy of military strategic superiority, the ACDA changed course and lost its initial significance. Nevertheless, arms limitation and disarmament are now such a specialized field in the grey area between political and military problems that they undoubtedly require an institutional apparatus. This becomes obvious from a quick look at the most important current negotiations.

[133]

It is the arms control and disarmament negotiations in Geneva on the reduction of strategic arms — START — and of intermediate-range nuclear weapons — INF — which attract the most attention since they represent the most important weapons issue at this time. However, just before the beginning of the START talks, which replaced the SALT negotiations rejected by the Reagan Administration, the USA announced a trade embargo against the Soviet Union. This was followed shortly after the talks had begun by Reagan's decision not to negotiate on the proposal for a complete ban on nuclear weapons. The effect on START's position was predictable. The United States was aiming at a massive reduction in Soviet land-based nuclear systems while securing further latitude for its own rearmament. According to American calculations, the START concept would be both unacceptable and disadvantageous for the Soviet Union as far as the ratio of warheads to targets (silos) was concerned. It would rise from 4.65:1 to 20:1, thus encouraging any predisposition for a first strike against the Soviet Union. This is a clear indication that, for the USA, the talks were no more than a facade, not intended to reach any conclusive results; rather they were to be a palliative to calm public opinion and the less experienced parliamentarians.

A similar observation can be made about the much exploited 'zero option' proposal regarding INF weapons. On 19 November 1981 the *Frankfurter Allgemeine Zeitung*, renowned for its critical attitude towards Soviet policy, commented that 'Moscow cannot accept it'. By any military yardstick the option cannot be a realistic one for the Russians. One should question, therefore, American motives in making the proposal. In view of the Administration's approach to arms negotiations, is it not rational to suggest that the Americans knew very well that the zero option could never be acceptable but used it as a tactic for achieving its purpose in procuring the eventual deployment of Cruise and Pershing II and strengthening its nuclear guard? The only options open to the USSR were either unconditional submission or the acceptance of failure in the START and INF negotiations. One suspects that the USA was more concerned with the deployment of its 572 intermediate-range missiles than in reducing the numbers of SS-20s and the outdated SS-4s and 5s, which cannot reach the US in any case.

The dual-track decision might be described as being 'dual' only in terms of its threat to the USSR on the one hand and as a means of deceiving the population of Western Europe as to the possible dangers on the other. The INF deployments help to enforce US military strategy despite reservations on the part of the West European governments. Three ways in which the USA can accomplish its strategic purpose would be by:

— linking START and INF in an effort to confuse the negotiating process, thereby allowing time for deployment;
— delaying the INF talks until the completion of deployment, i.e. by rejecting the inclusion of British and French systems in the talks, by seeking global reductions, by insisting on the scrapping of SS-20s, or by proposing any other unacceptable control measure in order to buy time;
— by making use of the special rights the United States has in the Federal Republic of Germany, which allow US forces to be equipped and armed irrespective of the German government's opinion.

The NATO dual-track decision is just as dangerous for Western Europe and the USA as it is for the Soviet Union, which has repeatedly announced counter-measures to be taken in the event of this decision being carried out. The measures in question are technically feasible and would have serious military consequences.

Negotiations on mutual and balanced force reduction (MBFR) are also extremely important for reducing military confrontation in Europe. They have been conducted in Vienna since 30 October 1973 without any definite result. They are aiming at a treaty on the reduction of ground and air forces which, on NATO's side, would cover West Germany and the Benelux countries and on the Warsaw Pact's side the GDR, Poland and Czechoslovakia. In this area, 979,000 Warsaw Pact soldiers face 991,000 NATO soldiers. At present, a withdrawal of 20,000 Soviet and 13,000 US soldiers during a first stage is being discussed, to be followed by a second stage run-down on both sides to 900,000 (700,000 and 200,000 air troops). Nothing has been achieved so far, because of different views on the actual numbers, on the kind of reduction to be undertaken ('attenuation' or withdrawal of complete units) and on the limitation of qualitative improvements in combat effectiveness, which could undermine the point of the negotiations.

The UN, both in Geneva and New York, are also involved with the issues. The Disarmament Committee in Geneva has been meeting since 1978, addressing itself to the questions of safeguards for non-nuclear states, a comprehensive disarmament treaty, a ban on radiological and chemical weapons and a complete nuclear weapon test ban. There are also the Disarmament Commission in New York with its special Committees working to set up a World Disarmament Conference and the Indian Ocean as a Zone of Peace, a Preparatory Committee for UN Special Sessions on Disarmament and a Scientific Committee on the Effects of Atomic Radiation (UNSCEAR). The Vienna-based International Atomic Energy Agency (IAEA) is responsible for monitoring the use of nuclear fuels and fission products for peaceful purposes and for ensuring that these materials are not being used secretly for the production of nuclear weapons.

Between 1978 and 1980, the US discontinued a number of important negotiations with the Soviet Union which have not been reactivated. They include:

— the American–Soviet–British negotiations on a complete and general nuclear weapon test ban;
— negotiations on the ban and elimination of chemical weapons;
— negotiations on the limitation of conventional arms exports;
— negotiations on the reduction of military activities in the Indian Ocean;
— negotiations on anti-satellite systems.

Successful negotiations in all these spheres would ensure a positive advance towards reducing the dangers inherent in the arms race. Yet almost two billion dollars are spent world-wide every day while the social needs of even the most highly developed countries cannot be met for, allegedly, financial reasons. Is it to be wondered that non-aligned countries are increasingly questioning the USA's and other nations' pre-occupation with achieving nuclear superiority?

Retired Admiral Noel Gayler, when addressing the Washington Press Club in February 1983, openly criticized President Reagan's policy in respect of land-based strategic missile systems. Gayler is not only a former Commander-in-Chief of the US Forces in the Pacific but also a former head of the National Security Agency, the most secret and highly technical US intelligence service. He cannot be accused of either a lack of professional knowledge or competence or of a pro-Soviet attitude. His ideas deserve careful consideration because they could indicate a way to resolve the complexities of US policy and the effect it is having on the unity of the Atlantic Alliance. Gayler said that nuclear weapons systems are, simply, of no military value and that employing them is effective neither on land nor at sea. America as well as the Soviet Union could easily destroy 'thousands' of their nuclear weapons and stop the production of new nuclear systems. He thought the Soviet Union was prepared to sign a nuclear agreement with the USA. Both powers needed at most only around a hundred nuclear weapons to provide an adequate mutual deterrence. Gayler stressed that there is no possible protection against nuclear weapons; civil defence is simply a waste of time, effort and money; that most politicians had not the faintest idea of the power and effects of nuclear weapons and that an opponent of nuclear weapons was by no means an enemy of the military, or of America.

His ideas provided important pointers for the future and deserve whole-hearted support. Coming from an established American military leader, they are of special value. They show clearly that the Reagan Administration is not America and that Weinberger does not represent the attitude of all groups of responsible military leaders. There are clear conclusions to be drawn from Gayler's statement:

firstly, a significant margin exists for radical arms control and disarmament measures which can be applied without endangering the security of the USA and its allies;

secondly, the Soviet Union can be respected as a negotiating partner with whom appropriate agreements can be concluded on the renunciation of further armament increases and with whom there can be cooperation and nuclear disarmament instead of confrontation and nuclear armament;

thirdly, it makes possible an immediate freeze on nuclear arms and a reduction in military spending. The next logical step after a freeze is arms reduction;

fourthly, by rejecting the strategy of nuclear warfare, one is not rejecting national defence as a military responsibility. To do so is not to challenge the role of the military but rather setting a pre-condition for its fulfilment;

fifthly, in Admiral Gayler's opinion, a radical reduction in strategic nuclear systems demands also the elimination of other nuclear systems deployed in Europe and other regions of the globe. They are as much a danger to the countries in which they are deployed as to the USA. Nuclear weapons should only be deployed in countries which already possess similar systems of their own;

finally, the renunciation of the nuclear warfare option, which is unacceptable to Western Europe, would help stabilize relations between NATO countries. It would make it easier for the governments as well as the populations of NATO countries to regard the Atlantic

Alliance as an institution representing their common security interests.

Our demand: disarmament now!

There is a growing concern among a number of military men and responsible scientists that leading politicians ignore the dangers of nuclear war and, were it to come, believe they could survive in underground shelters and headquarters. Nuclear weapons, however, are neither 'super-bombs' nor 'weapons' in the traditional sense of the word. As a means for the massive destruction of all life, their effect cannot be limited to 'enemy' territory. Scientists fear that, even in the (unlikely) case of a limited nuclear exchange, the release of nitrogen oxides and carbon dioxide would have disastrous world-wide consequences. The full effects of the destruction of the ozone layer and the triggering of a 'hot-house effect', which would drastically increase average temperatures, cannot be fully calculated. If power stations were bombed, the resulting radioactive contamination would last for centuries, without respect for state or continental boundaries. Now the scientists have warned against a 'nuclear winter', which will be caused by the dust cloud that will rise into the atmosphere after the nuclear explosions and blot out the sun's rays. This will lead to a rapid and long-lasting drop in temperature all over the globe to levels well below freezing point.

Scientists, doctors and artists are not alone in their objections to the manner in which politicians and others play down the effects of nuclear war. We whose job it is to estimate and understand war and weapons and their consequences, cannot stand by idly and see irresponsible judgements being made. No one, not even so-called experts, can really estimate the full effect of mass nuclear explosions. No one can assess their cumulative effect or the side- and after-effects which would follow. Without taking into account the catastrophic consequences of the destruction of nuclear power stations, a calculation of the known effects shows that *all* human life would be endangered by an exchange of nuclear weapons. It must therefore be the duty of responsible people who know the truth to ensure that the facts are made known to the general public. An awareness of the true effects of nuclear war must be advertised, not kept secret, if our society is to survive.

It has to be recognized that illusions exist, and not only in respect of the effects of nuclear weapons. Many politicians and, above all,

[138]

citizens are unaware of the dangers which exist in the political, military and technological fields and which could lead to a nuclear holocaust; the chances of this happening are increasing. We believe it is necessary, therefore:

— to break the exclusive monopoly of knowledge by the few about military facts and figures and make military policy understandable and more accessible to those involved in the democratic decision-making process;
— to expose a policy which rationalizes military power and the use of nuclear weapons as being a primary and suitable means for achieving prescribed objectives, instead of recognising the inherent risks involved and the fact that it would be madness to use them, even as last resort methods, in peacekeeping terms;
— to stress the economic and social consequences of, and to call public attention to, the inter-relationship between growing military expenditure and cuts in public welfare spending, subsidies for civilian industries, research and development aid.

The necessity for taking these steps is especially relevant at this time since it is not only doubtful whether new treaties on arms limitation can be signed but it appears increasingly likely that existing treaties and agreements could be violated or even cancelled. Attempts to mislead public opinion and the less informed politicians through the misrepresentation of the facts, and the lack of willingness on the part of the USA and some of its NATO partners to negotiate, are added factors in the lack of progress in seeking arms limitation.

Those who promote such armament programmes as the development of the first strike weapons, which have a destabilizing effect on the strategic balance, while at the same time pursuing illusions about non-existent effective anti-ballistic missile systems, must be opposed. Henry Kissinger, among others, would like to do without them as they would overcharge the deterrence system and further confuse matters. The race for a functional ABM system would be on and one wonders what would be the effect if the Soviet Union got there first!

A continuation of the arms race must not be permitted. What is needed instead is a constructive dialogue between East and West, bringing in its wake a gradual removal of the threat as each sees it. Politicians who cannot understand this have no business to be in governments or even parliaments. The peace movement has the task of forcing politicians to see reason and of confronting the armament industry lobbyists with a determined and informed electorate. It is necessary to explore every avenue within the democratic system by which the present course of events can be resolutely stopped and the confrontation removed. In this context, as Sidney D. Drell commented to the *International Herald Tribune*:

> Looking ahead through the 1980s, the challenge is to continue to make deterrence work while striving to reduce the nuclear threat and, eventually, remove it altogether. I identify four essential steps that would contribute to a saner and safer world.
> — The United States must reject the dangerous illusion of survivable and winnable nuclear wars. Weapons decisions should be based simply on the criterion of maintaining a secure and reliable deterrent, and not on any further war-fighting requirements that are generally as limitless as they are unrealistic.
> — We must create an informed and responsible public constituency which insists that its elected officials give arms control at least as high a priority as increased arms for national security — and makes that concern felt at the voting booth.
> — Americans and Russians must negotiate with urgency and in good faith and, at the same time, show restraint in weapons programmes. We must continue to call for concrete evidence that the negotiations, as well as new weapons programmes, are consistent with the agreed principle.
> — We must return the nuclear debate to a fundamental moral level. It is not enough for society to focus on the latest numbers and models of nuclear weapons. We have to remember what they can actually do. What is at stake is the survival of civilization as we know it.[5]

Disarmament will not come about on its own. It will be achieved only as a result of determined and persistent actions and initiatives. The duty and task of those with expert knowledge of the problems related to nuclear weapon strategies — generals and others who work for peace — is to supply the arguments and support the actions of those whose purpose is to secure peace for our world. More than ever before do we need to act with resolution to bring about disarmament. There are more realistic ways to set about it than by indulging in the old illusion that security depends upon military superiority. Anyone understanding the principles of modern war, which we can claim to do, knows one thing for sure — nuclear victory is impossible!

Appendix 1

Vienna meeting of former NATO and Warsaw Pact generals, 15-18 May 1984

This meeting was the culmination of two years of preparation which began in Washington DC in June 1982 with a meeting between Brigadier Michael Harbottle and USSR Ambassador Anatoly Dobrynin. By that time the NATO Generals' group for Peace and Disarmament had been in existence for one year and had already addressed memoranda on the dangers of the continuing arms race to the Madrid Conference on European Security and Cooperation (1981), the Foreign and Defence Ministers of NATO (1981) and the Second UN Special Session on Disarmament (1982).

More experienced people than we believed that agreement for a meeting would take anything up to five years to accomplish. The fact that it took less than two years from the time of the first approaches indicates the extent of the sense of urgency which existed in people's minds by the end of 1983, creating a climate for such a meeting. In the event, a high measure of cooperation between the generals' group and Moscow established the parameters of our Agenda and ensured the participation of representatives from all the Warsaw Pact countries.

The agenda for the meeting was concerned with the overall issue of East-West relations and security, and addressed itself to:

(a) the factors which increase the dangers of the arms race and their effect on world security;

(b) the steps needed to end the arms race;

(c) appropriate confidence building measures and their application to arms control and disarmament;

(d) non-provocative defence as an alternative strategy.

Each item on the agenda was allotted at least half a day for its

[141]

consideration.

The strength of the meeting was in the attitude and approach of each participant. We were fourteen individuals, not two opposing groups — the East Europeans have no group structure like ours. We addressed ourselves to the subject for discussion as soldiers. At no time during the three and a half days were we diverted by political or ideological argument. We were questioned at the end by the media as to how it was that two such opposing ideological groups could jointly produce and unanimously agree a Final Statement of such a nature. Each participant emphasized that we were soldiers and that we had been discussing military matters in military terms; therefore there had been no problem in agreeing the contents of the Statement since they made military sense.

The initiative received the support which one had hoped it would. It opened the way for further meetings, not only of the generals (planned for May 1985), but also for other like categories of experienced people — such as former diplomats, the media, those in business and industry. The success of the meeting was due to all those concerned with its planning, to the participants and all who were concerned with its organization and management; not least the governments of the Warsaw Pact countries, without whose interest and approval it is unlikely that the meeting could have taken place.

The following generals attended the meeting.

For the NATO countries: General Georgios Koumanakos (*Greece*); General Nino Pasti (*Italy*); Generaal-Majoor M. N. von Meyenfeldt (*Netherlands*); General Johan Christie (*Norway*); General Joao Lima (*Portugal*); Brigadier (General) Michael Harbottle (*United Kingdom*).

For the WTO countries: Lt. General Petar Iliev (*Bulgaria*); Colonel General Samual Kodaj (*Czechoslovakia*); Major General Kurt Lohberger (*GDR*); Major General Tibor Saardy (*Hungary*); General M. Naszkowski (*Poland*); General Ion Tutoveanu (*Romania*); Colonel General Alexander N. Ponomarev and Major General Taer A. Simonyan (*USSR*).

The Final Statement is printed below.

MEETING OF RETIRED NATO/WTO GENERALS
Vienna 15–18 May 1984
THE FINAL STATEMENT

A meeting of former generals of NATO and Warsaw Treaty countries took place in Vienna, Austria, from 15–18 May 1984.

The NATO members included former senior officers of the armed forces from Great Britain, Greece, Italy, the Netherlands, Norway and Portugal.

The Warsaw Treaty countries were represented by former generals from Bulgaria, Czechoslovakia, the GDR, Hungary, Poland, Romania and the USSR, who are presently actively involved in the activities of Peace Committees, War Veterans Committees and other public organizations and movements in their respective countries.

This unprecedented meeting was the first of its kind. The fact of it being held at a time that is difficult for the cause of peace, and that it was attended by persons of different political persuasions who lived through the trying years of the Second World War, is itself highly significant. The discussions they had were based on a common concern for the security of Europe which is their common home and which has experienced two wars during this century. They consider that they have a responsibility to direct all their efforts to maintaining peace on their continent.

The meeting bears witness not only to the growing concern in many sections of European public opinion with the destinies of Europe and the world, but also to the resolve to take joint action to halt the nuclear arms race and to prevent the nuclear catastrophe by all means which are available to the general public.

The participants in the meeting agreed that they can and must use their professional influence to support the efforts of those representing European and international public opinion to resolve such problems as:

[143]

— ridding Europe of all nuclear weapons and other weapons of mass destruction; among other ways, by creating nuclear free zones in Europe;
— prevention of the militarization of outer space;
— promotion of general disarmament;
— strengthening of confidence building measures and the return to détente, good neighbourliness and cooperation.

It was also stressed at the meeting that the resumption of INF talks at Geneva is not only desirable but necessary. At the same time, participants at the meeting comprehended the position of the Soviet Union that resumption of negotiations can only be possible if there is a return to the position that existed in Europe before the deployment of Cruise and Pershing II missiles. There was also a consensus view that when determining the balance between nuclear medium weapons of NATO and USSR, the nuclear weapons of the United Kingdom and France should be taken into consideration.

Participants also agreed with the necessity to bring into public debate and to encourage the contribution that the public can make to the achievement of the following important measures:

1. A treaty on non use of military force and the maintenance of peaceful relations between the countries of NATO and WTO;

2. Commitment of all nuclear states to non first use of nuclear weapons;

3. Agreement on a freeze of all development, testing, production and deployment of weapons of mass destruction;

4. Agreement on removal from Europe of chemical weapons and the destruction of all stocks of chemical weapons in the world;

5. The freezing of military budgets and to decrease them step by step;

6. More careful consideration given to major proposals submitted by governments on arms control and disarmament;

7. Regular consultations between European states at all possible levels concerning the problems of European security as a contribution to the implementation of the above measures.

Participants expressed their firm support for the goals and objectives of the Stockholm Conference as well as their conviction that its results could contribute to the peaceful future of Europe and the world. They also agreed on possible contributions that the general public could make towards confidence building measures, e.g.:

(a) to broaden involvement and interaction between different professional and other groups, such as that entered into at this meeting in Vienna;

(b) to encourage the media to play a more responsible role; in reporting the facts of the arms race and underplaying those aspects which excite rather than diminish distrust;

(c) to extend the discussion of new ideas and proposals concerned with disarmament, including alternative defence and security strategies.

Finally, the participants agreed that the future of the peoples of Europe can be based only on the principles of equality and equal security for all peoples in the continent, bearing in mind that the solution of this vital problem depends primarily on themselves. They realised that European security is linked with the security of other parts of the world and that everything possible has to be done to remove the seeds of conflict in areas like Central America, the Middle East and South East Asia.

The former senior officers of NATO and WTO countries evaluated most highly this first experience of holding such a meeting, which took place in an atmosphere of constructive dialogue, and expressed their interest in the continuation of this new and useful form of cooperation.

Appendix 2

[.....]

In its memorandum to the 1982 UN Second Special Session on Disarmament, the group of Generals put forward a formula which outlines the steps they believe are practical and realistic. Set in sequence, the steps are these:

1 *A Freeze*. So long as negotiations for disarmament continue under the shadow of a continuing arms race, little if anything substantial is likely to be achieved. A halt to all development, production and deployment of nuclear weapons would provide a clear start from which subsequent steps could proceed. *A Renunciation* of first use of nuclear weapons by all nuclear weapon states and a formal agreement entered into by those states.

2 *Independent Initiatives*. Mutual steps taken independently and simultaneously by the nuclear powers could be: USSR: dismantlement of SS-20 system; USA: discontinuance of the MX programme; UK: cancellation of its Trident programme; France: cancellation of its independent deterrence programme. Such a mutual approach linked to 1 above would ease tension and create confidence, leading to progress towards other disarmament and weapon control agreements.

3 Nations having nuclear weapons located in other countries should agree to withdraw them and all nuclear nations should renounce foreign deployment of such weapons.

4 The establishment of nuclear free zones in Europe, covering both sides of the NATO–Warsaw Pact 'curtain'. Zones in the Baltic and Balkans have been proposed and in January 1983 the Soviet Union proposed a zone for the central front. These land zones could be augmented by zones of peace in the main oceanic areas of the world.

This would extend the restrictions to sub service nuclear weapons and carriers (submarines) in those areas.

5 Strategic arms stocks to be reduced to the minimum necessary for the threat of retaliation. Tactical weapon systems to be abolished.

6 Conventional armed forces and their equipments to be cut to a size consistent with national defence requirements.

7 The eventual military disengagement in Europe, by which the foreign troops stationed there under existing NATO and Warsaw Pact arrangements would return home. This should be followed by the dissolution of the two alliances as military entities, though they would be permitted to continue as treaty alliances until such time as they were deemed to be no longer essential.

Together, this package constitutes a comprehensive approach to disarmament. The Generals believe that in the sequence that has been suggested, every stage could be negotiated without any loss of security or essential safeguards. The disengagement and dissolution of NATO and the Warsaw Treaty Organisation comes at the end of the sequence but it is only realistic to expect this to happen after the other stages have been completed. Within each stage, one side or the other may be required to take an initiative which might constitute a temporary risk but taking a risk for peace can be better than taking a risk for war.

Source: Generals for Peace and Disarmament, *Ten Questions Answered*, London/Banbury, 1983, pp. 30–2

References

Generals for Peace and Disarmament — a Survey

1. *Die Zeit*, 1 May 1981
2. *Stern*, 6, 1982, p. 10
3. Interview with General Nino Pasti, *Neue Zeit*, 40, 1978, p. 9
4. *Frankfurter Allgemeine Zeitung*, 7 September 1981
5. W. Hessler, *Operation Survival*, New York, 1949, p. 39
6. R. Steinmetz, *Soziologie des Krieges*, Leipzig, 1929, pp. 18ff.
7. Stature of the United Nations, *Keesings' Archiv der Gegenwart*, Bonn, 26 June 1945, p. 289
8. W. S. Churchill, *The Second World War*, vol. 6, pt. 2, London, 1954
9. *Wehrkunde*, 6, 1970, p. 281
10. *Stern*, 46, 1981, p. 82
11. R. Nixon, 'Unsere Trümpfe spielen', *Welt am Sonntag*, 29 August 1982
12. H.-J. Müller-Borchert, *Guerilla im Industriestaat*, Hamburg, 1973, pp. 53–4
13. C. B. Otley, 'Militarism and the social affiliations of the British Army élite', *Armed Forces and Society*, Paris/The Hague, 1968, p. 89; *Schriftenreihe Innere Führung*, 29, Bonn, 1977
14. A. Sanguinetti, 'Es ist die Aufgabe der Europäer, ihre Verbündeten wieder zur Vernunft zu bringen', *Blätter für deutsche und internationale Politik* (Rüstungs-wettlauf), 4, Cologne, 1981, p. 397
15. Lord Louis Mountbatten, 'Über den Atomkrieg', *Ist der nukleare Rüstungs-wettlauf vermeidbar*, Fürth, 1981, p. 130
16. A. Sanguinetti, op. cit., p. 298
17. *Yearbook of the United Nations 1961*, New York, 1961, pp. 30–1
18. Pastoral Letter of the National Conference of Catholic Bishops on War and Peace, Washington, DC, 1982
19. 'Automare Rüstung', *Bulletin des Presse- und Informationsamtes der Bundes-regierung*, Bonn, 7 May 1958; *Evangelischer Pressedienst*, 18 March 1958
20. Monsignore Dr R. P. Bär, 'Haltung von kirchlichen Gruppen in den Niederlanden zu Fragen von Krieg und Frieden', *NATO-Brief*, 1, Brussels, 1982, p. 27

The Reagan Administration's Confrontation Policy

1. C. S. Gray and K. Payne, 'Victory is Possible' *Foreign Policy*, 39, Summer 1980
2. Election Mainfesto of the Republican Party, quoted in *Defense Monitor*, 3, 1981, p. 3
3. *The Times*, 9 June 1982
4. Speech to the Foreign Policy Association, New York, *Amerika-Dienst*, Bonn/Bad Godesberg, 15 July 1981
5. Ibid.
6. Speech to the Council on Foreign Relations in New York, *Wireless Bulletin from Washington*, 201, Bonn, 22 October 1981, p. 11
7. *International Herald Tribune*, 29 January 1982
8. Speech to the Bar Association of New Orleans, *Amerika-Dienst*, Bonn/Bad Godesberg, 19 August 1981, p. 16
9. *Wireless Bulletin from Washington*, 177, Bonn, 17 September 1981, p. 20
10. *Süddeutsche Zeitung*, 20 October 1982; *Die Welt*, 20 October 1982
11. Ibid.
12. *International Herald Tribune*, 21 January 1983; *Neue Zürcher Zeitung*, 22 January 1983
13. See, for example: 'Tories wage secret war on peace campaigners', *New Statesman*, 31 January 1983; 'Strategic Tory attack on the nuclear disarmers', *The Guardian*, 14 February 1983; 'Tories zero in on the "latter-day appeasers"', *The Times*, 2 March 1983; 'Revival of Political Warfare', *The Times*, 1 March 1983
14. *Newsweek*, 30 March 1981
15. G. F. Kennan, *Im Schatten der Atombombe. Eine Analyse der Amerikanisch-sowjetischen Beziehungen von 1947 bis heute*, Cologne, 1982
16. *USIS Bulletin*, 10 February 1983
17. G. F. Kennan, 'Rede anlässlich der Verleihung des Friedenspreises des deutschen Buchhandels am 10.10.1982', *Süddeutsche Zeitung*, 11 October 1982
18. C. Krause, 'Was ist militärische Bedrohung?', *Die Neue Gesellschaft*, 4, Bonn, 1982, pp. 323–4
19. *Frankfurter Rundschau*, 3 February 1983; *SIPRI Yearbook*, London. 1982, p. 277, gives the figures as 7,032 (USA) and 6,848 (USSR)
20. *Der Tagesspiegel*, 7 September 1982
21. 'Now is the Time to Talk to Moscow', interview with M. D. Schulman, *Newsweek*, 20 April 1982, p. 60
22. C. Krause, op. cit.; idem, 'Plus/Minus dreiunddreissig Divisionen. Stimmt der militärische Kräftevegleich?' *Die Neue Gesellschaft*, 11, 1982, pp. 1078–9
23. *Christian Science Monitor*, 7 November 1980
24. *International Herald Tribune*, 8 March 1983
25. *International Herald Tribune*, 21 January 1983
26. W. Hahlweg, *Guerilla-Krieg ohne Fronten*, Stuttgart, 1968, p. 195
27. Ibid., p. 196
28. USA War Office (ed.), *Special Warfare US Army*, Washington, 1962, p. 8

29. J. F. Kennedy, 'Rede auf der Gedenkfeier für den polnischen Freiheitshelden General Pulaski in Buffalo', *Der Tag*, 16 October 1962
30. *Special Warfare US Army*, p. 95
31. *International Herald Tribune*, 20 July 1982
32. 'Final Agreement from the Conference on Security and Cooperation in Europe', *Bundestags-Drucksache*, No. 7/3867, Bonn, 23 July 1975

Is Suicide a Defence?

1. *International Security*, vol. 2, no. 2, 1977
2. *Die Welt*, 25 January 1983
3. *Die Überlebenden werden die Toten beneiden. Materialien des Hamburger 'Medizinischen Kongresses zur Verhinderung des Atomkrieges' vom 19/20 September 1981*, Cologne, 1982, pp. 109ff.
4. *International Herald Tribune*, Paris, 21 June 1983
5. *Wireless Bulletin from Washington*, 18 June 1981
6. C. S. Gray and K. Payne, op. cit., p. 14
7. 'FM 100-1', *The Army*, August 1981, p. 4
8. Quoted by Ege and Wenger in *Le Monde Diplomatique*, Paris, February 1983, pp. 12–13
9. Ibid.
10. *Foreign Affairs*, New York, Winter 1982/83
11. G. La Rocque, 'How a Nuclear War in Europe Would Be Fought', in H. W. Tromp and G. La Rocque, *Nuclear War in Europe*, Gröningen, 1982, p. 25
12. *The Times*, 7 March 1983
13. *International Herald Tribune*, 25 March 1982
14. *International Herald Tribune*, 8 September 1982
15. A. Mechtersheimer, *Rüstung und Frieden*, Munich, 1982, p. 24
16. Ibid., p. 147
17. G. La Rocque, op. cit., pp. 26ff.
18. Ibid., p. 29
19. Robert Scheer, *With Enough Shovels: Reagan, Bush and Nuclear War*, New York, 1982, pp. 18, 138–40
20. *International Herald Tribune*, 25 March 1982
21. Review in *Süddeutsche Zeitung*, 5/6 June 1982, p. 102
22. *Die Überlebenden werden die Toten beneiden*, pp. 47–8
23. Ibid., p. 221
24. *International Herald Tribune*, 16 August 1982

Towards a Military Policy Serving Peace

1. K. von Clausewitz, *Vom Kriege*, Bonn, 1952, p. 245
2. Quoted from E. Abel, *13 Tage vor dem 3. Weltkreig*, Vienna/Munich, 1966, pp. 278–9

3. G. Bastian, *Freiden schaffen — Gedanken zur Sicher heitspolitik*, Munich, 1983, pp. 166, 186ff.
4. D. S. Lutz, 'Von SALT zu START — Forderungen an eine verloren geglaubte Sache', *Die Neue Gesellschaft*, 7, Bonn, 1982, pp. 671-3; *Der Palme-Bericht. Bericht der unabhängigen Kommission für Abrüstung und Sicherheit*, Berlin, 1982

Disarmament — the Need of the Moment

1. UN office of Public Information (ed.), 'Final Document of Assembly Session on Disarmament, 23 May-1 July 1978', New York, 1978, p. 4
2. *Department of State Bulletin*, vol. 49, no. 1253, Washington, 17 July 1963, pp. 1-2, 4
3. *Archiv der Gegenwart*, 42, Bonn/Vienna/Zurich, 1972, pp. 17, 127
4. *International Herald Tribune*, 2 July 1982
5. *International Herald Tribune*, 14 September 1982